PRAISE FOR
Hell? Yes!

"In *Hell? Yes!* Robert Jeffress approaches the Goliath-like issues of our time with the calm, dead-eye aim of a contemporary David. If you want an encounter with the truth, read this book! It is so timely for this generation."
—JOSH D. MCDOWELL, author and speaker

"I have no doubt that many will come to a place of hope and will find peace for their souls as they read *Hell? Yes!*"
—DENNIS JERNIGAN, author of *Giant Killers,* song writer,
and Doxology recording artist

PRAISE FOR
I Want More!

"*I Want More!* weighs the limited experience of the average believer against the dynamic promise of the Holy Spirit's work and power in his or her life. Robert Jeffress reminds us that Spirit-charged living is not the result of an occasional high-voltage worship experience, but rather a daily reliance on the 'Generator'—the Holy Spirit—working on behalf of regenerated men and women. If you want more, this is a book that answers the cry of your heart."
—JACK GRAHAM, pastor of Prestonwood Baptist Church,
Plano, Texas

"The reader of *I Want More!* steps into a chapel of warm reverence where the Father's invitation to come to Him is explained not in theological jargon but with an assuring explanation. The life-changing work of the Holy

Spirit is neither hyped nor hidden, simply made available to those who seek His presence."

—HOWARD G. HENDRICKS, Distinguished Professor
and chairman, Center for Christian Leadership, Dallas
Theological Seminary

PRAISE FOR
The Solomon Secrets

"Robert Jeffress is a talented pastor and gifted writer with a heart for God. Once again he has done a masterful job in presenting practical principles that every man and woman can apply. *The Solomon Secrets* is filled with pure gold. So enjoy the hunt for treasure as Robert helps unlock the vast riches of God's wisdom found in Proverbs."

—DR. ED YOUNG, senior pastor, Second Baptist Church,
Houston, Texas

"Dr. Jeffress's…book is a compilation of hard-hitting, practical wisdom for daily living. You will profit greatly from studying *The Solomon Secrets*. The study guide included in the book will aid small-group study of this helpful volume."

—DR. KEN HEMPHILL, president, Southwestern Baptist
Theological Seminary

GRACE GONE WILD!

ALSO BY ROBERT JEFFRESS

Coming Home
The Solomon Secrets
Hearing the Master's Voice
When Forgiveness Doesn't Make Sense
I Want More!
Hell? Yes!

ROBERT JEFFRESS

GRACE GONE WILD!

GETTING A GRIP ON GOD'S AMAZING GIFT

WATERBROOK

GRACE GONE WILD!

All Scripture quotations, unless otherwise indicated, are taken from the *New American Standard Bible®*. (NASB). © Copyright The Lockman Foundation 1960, 1962, 1963, 1968, 1971, 1972, 1973, 1975, 1977, 1995. Used by permission. (www.Lockman.org). Scripture quotations marked (KJV) are taken from the *King James Version.* Scripture quotations marked (NIV) are taken from the *Holy Bible, New International Version®*. Copyright © 1973, 1978, 1984 by International Bible Society. Used by permission of Zondervan Publishing House. All rights reserved. Scripture quotations marked (NLT) are taken from the *Holy Bible, New Living Translation,* copyright © 1996. Used by permission of Tyndale House Publishers, Inc., Wheaton, Illinois 60189. All rights reserved.

Italics in Scripture quotations reflect the author's added emphasis.

Details in some anecdotes and stories have been changed to protect the identities of the persons involved.

Trade Paperback ISBN 978-1-57856-521-4
eBook ISBN 978-0-307-83069-2

Published in the United States by WaterBrook, an imprint of Random House, a division of Penguin Random House LLC.

WATERBROOK® and its deer colophon are registered trademarks of Penguin Random House LLC.

Library of Congress Cataloging-in-Publication Data
Jeffress, Robert, 1955–
    Grace gone wild! : getting a grip on God's amazing gift / Robert Jeffress.—1st ed.
    p. cm.
    Includes bibliographical references.
    ISBN 1-57856-521-9
    1. Grace (Theology). I. Title.
BT761.3.J44 2005
234—dc22

                                                              2005014142

Printed in the United States of America

SPECIAL SALES WaterBrook books are available at special quantity discounts when purchased in bulk by corporations, organizations, and special-interest groups. Custom imprinting or excerpting can also be done to fit special needs. For information, please email specialmarketscms@penguinrandomhouse.com.

9 8 7 6 5 4 3

*To my trusted mentor and faithful friend Dr. Howard G. Hendricks,
whose impact on my life for the past thirty years is one of the
clearest evidences of God's grace. Thanks, "Prof."*

Contents

Acknowledgments

Thank you...

Steve Cobb and the wonderful team at WaterBrook—for your support, especially when it comes to tough messages like *Grace Gone Wild!* and *Hell? Yes!*

Bruce Nygren, Alice Crider, and Jennifer Lonas—for suggesting ways to "soften the blow" without compromising the message.

Sealy Yates, my agent and friend for the past decade—for your valued insights.

Carrilyn Baker—for your persistence in tracking down the dozens of sources for this book...and you're still smiling!

GRACE GONE WILD!

UNDERSTANDING
GOOD GRACE

CHAPTER ONE

The Grace Escape

Brian Gilmore desperately needed some grace, but few in his church were willing to offer him any. For the past four years, Brian had led the men's ministry program at Grace Church. Although Brian was employed as a software specialist for a local accounting firm, his real passion was discipling men. He devoted lunch hours, evenings after work, and Saturdays to small-group Bible studies, personal mentoring, and marital counseling—which is how Brian met Susan and Randy Johnston.

Susan, a committed Christian, had finally persuaded her husband, Randy, to start attending Grace Church. Randy had very little interest in spiritual matters, but he attended Grace to appease his wife and, perhaps, to expand his client base in the increasingly competitive cancer-insurance business. So Susan was pleasantly surprised when Randy signed up for a men's small-group Bible study that Brian was leading.

Over the next few months, Brian could sense by some of Randy's blunt and often sarcastic comments that he and his wife, Susan, were struggling in their relationship. So he asked if Randy would be open to the three of them getting together over coffee to discuss their issues. Randy agreed, hoping that Brian might be the much-needed ally he was seeking to help get Susan off his back. Perhaps a few strong words about submission from a neutral third party would do the trick.

But the sessions did not turn out as Randy expected. Instead, Brian directed most of his comments to Randy, encouraging him to love his wife "as Christ also loved the church" (Ephesians 5:25). About two sessions of that kind of advice was all Randy needed before he bolted. He not only refused to attend any more counseling sessions with Brian, but he stopped attending Grace Church altogether. However, Susan asked Brian if she might continue meeting with him so she might better understand how to be "a godly wife."

During subsequent visits Brian confided that he, too, knew what it was like to be "unequally yoked" with someone who did not share his spiritual commitment. Although Brian's wife, Cindy, was a Christian who attended Grace Church regularly and made sure that their children did as well, she did not share Brian's enthusiasm for ministry, at least from Brian's perspective. She thought her husband should be spending his time after work and on Saturdays with her and their two small children instead of with strangers. In his spiritual journal Brian identified with the apostle Paul, who ministered faithfully in spite of his "thorn in the flesh" (2 Corinthians 12:7). As far as Brian was concerned, Cindy was his thorn in the flesh. He could empathize completely with Susan's feelings about being in a spiritually mismatched marriage, which explains why they so easily and quickly fell in love.

Within a few months, Susan's husband was fed up with the situation and moved out, and Brian left his wife and children and moved in with Susan. The pastor and elders at Grace Church knew the Bible demanded that they confront Brian and ask him to resign as the men's ministry coordinator. However, when they met with him, they were unprepared for his response.

"You have no idea how hard I worked to keep my marriage together. But from day one I knew that my marriage to Cindy was a mistake. For the sake of the kids, I tried to do the best I could to keep our marriage together. However, I don't believe that God would want me to be trapped in a loveless marriage the rest of my life just because of one mistake. Which one of you has never made a mistake? Would you want to spend the rest of your life paying for that mistake?" Brian asked.

He continued, "I've asked God to forgive me, and His Word promises that He has. I feel perfectly at peace with my decision to build a new life with Susan. After all, we live under grace, not law."

Cindy Gilmore, Brian's abandoned wife, was sick and tired of hearing about grace. When she felt she could no longer endure watching her husband carry on an illicit affair with someone else's wife, she confided in her closest friend, Beth. "I don't know what to do. Every time I confront Brian about his relationship with Susan, he tells me that he needs time to sort out his feelings. Am I supposed to just stand by and watch him destroy two families? Am I supposed to risk contracting a sexually transmitted disease because of his unfaithfulness? What kind of message is this sending to our children?"

Beth listened sympathetically and waited until Cindy had run out of steam before she responded. Then, in a comforting voice, she said, "I know this is terribly difficult and unfair. I'm sure I don't understand the pain you're feeling, and I wish there were some way I could take it away. But, Cindy, think about all the unfair treatment Christ endured on the cross for us. And He asks us as His followers to do the same for others. Grace means giving people what they need, not what they deserve. Yes, what Brian has done is wrong, and he deserves divorce. But he needs forgiveness."

———

Pastor Jerry Steakley was not in a forgiving mood on Easter Sunday morning. For the past several years, both attendance and giving at Elmwood Baptist Church had been declining. Pastor Jerry and his small staff were finding it increasingly difficult to enlist volunteers to teach Sunday school or work in the nursery during the worship service. They were continually met with excuses from church members, such as "We would love to serve, but because we spend a lot of time at our lake house, we're not here that often" or "Our child has joined a traveling soccer team, and that keeps us from being in church regularly."

To add insult to injury, some of those members—when they *were* in town—had been attending Living Waters Fellowship, a new nondenominational church that emphasized freedom in Christ. This included freedom from the stifling structure and demands of traditional churches that were "more interested in their own growth than the spiritual growth of their members," as Living Waters' pastor Chip Bingham had said in a recent message that had circulated via cassette tape among some of Elmwood Baptist's disgruntled members. "One thing we will promise you here at Living Waters is that no one will ever tell you how much you should give to this church, and no one will jump down your throat for missing a Sunday. We want you to be here because you want to be here. We want you to give out of joy, not duty," Pastor Chip promised. That sure sounded good to some members of Elmwood Baptist who were growing weary of the constant haranguing from the pulpit about attendance and giving.

The breaking point for Pastor Jerry came when he was driving to church on Easter Sunday morning and passed by the local tennis courts. To his astonishment, the courts were filled with teenagers and their parents—including some of his members—who were involved in a tennis tournament rather than being in church! During his Easter message that day, Pastor Jerry let loose: "Can you imagine the disciples, when asked by the women to come see the empty tomb, responding, 'Sorry, but we have a tennis tournament today' or 'Sorry, but we're going to our lake house today. May we drop by the grave next week?' No wonder the church is so anemic today!" the pastor bellowed.

That Easter Sunday was also the breaking point for the deacons of Elmwood Baptist. The following Tuesday night at their monthly meeting, the chairman, whose child had been participating in the tennis tournament, said, "Pastor, there is a growing discontent in our church about the negative tone of your sermons. You keep pressuring people to attend more and give more. Maybe if they were being fed spiritually, they would want to come. If they felt that we were more interested in their spiritual growth than our numerical growth, they would also give more. You are too legalistic in your approach. Remember, Pastor, we live under grace, not law."

All three of these scenarios represent a perversion of God's most cherished gift to His children: grace.

"For by grace you have been saved by faith," we recite.

"Amazing grace, how sweet the sound!" we sing.

"We live under grace," we claim.

Grace is part of the basic vocabulary in the Christianese language we speak. Unfortunately, many Christians today are abusing God's amazing gift of grace. They have perverted God's undeserved gift of forgiveness and promise of eternal life into a license for immorality, self-indulgence, and uninvolvement in God's kingdom. And in the process they are robbing themselves of the joy that comes from obeying God.

But God is not the only Person being victimized by the abuse of grace. You, too, have probably been on the receiving end of bad grace at one time or another:

- A close friend repeatedly criticizes you behind your back. You confide to someone your desire to confront your friend but are reminded that grace means being willing to "turn the other cheek."
- You catch your mate red-handed in an adulterous relationship. Through many tears, he confesses his mistake and begs your forgiveness, which you grant. Two months later you discover the affair is continuing. Not wanting to subject yourself or your children to this kind of dysfunctional home, you contemplate divorce but are reminded that grace means a willingness to forgive "seventy times seven."
- As a member of the leadership team at your church, you are concerned when a fellow leader is accused of a serious moral failing. You feel strongly that he should resign his position, at least until the issue is resolved. But you feel like a lone voice crying in the wilderness. You are reminded that grace means being unwilling to "judge lest you be judged."

GRACE UNDER THE MICROSCOPE

What exactly is grace? You have probably heard one or more of these definitions:

Grace is *God's Riches At Christ's Expense.*

Grace is the unmerited favor of God.

Grace is God giving us what we cannot earn.

But trying to formulate a precise definition of *grace* is like trying to define a rainbow for someone who has been blind from birth. "A rainbow is a mixture of moisture and dust in the atmosphere that, when illuminated

by the sun, reflects…." That doesn't quite capture the brilliance of a rainbow, does it? The only way to truly appreciate a rainbow is to see its beauty
with your own eyes. Similarly, grace must be experienced before it can be
more fully comprehended.

One of my favorite illustrations of grace is from the story of a social
worker named Henry Moorehouse who lived in the very worst of slum dis-
tricts in London, England, in the 1800s.

One evening as he was walking home, Moorehouse saw a little girl
carrying a pitcher of milk. Suddenly she fell, and the pitcher slipped out of
her hands and shattered. As the milk flowed into the gutter, the little girl
began to sob uncontrollably.

"Honey, don't cry," said Moorehouse as he helped her get up. But the
tears would not stop.

"I'll get a whipping from my mommy," the girl said between sobs.

"No, you won't. I'll help you put the pitcher back together again,"
Moorehouse assured her.

Suddenly the tears stopped, because the girl had seen other broken
pitchers repaired. But every time it looked as if Moorehouse would suc-
ceed, the pitcher would fall apart again. After several unsuccessful attempts,
the girl began crying again.

In the end, Moorehouse lifted the girl in his arms and carried her to a
crockery store, where he bought her a brand-new pitcher. Then he carried
her to the store where she had purchased the milk and paid to have the
pitcher filled once more. Finally, he carried her home.

Then Moorehouse asked the little girl if she thought her mother would
still whip her.

"No sir," she smiled. "This pitcher is much nicer than the one we had
before."[1]

God has done something even greater than this for us. Although we
were originally created in His likeness, sin shattered His image within us.

We can try to mend that image through good works and religious ritual, but we are broken beyond repair.

However, in a burst of undeserved generosity, God offers to give us a brand-new nature that He purchased for us at the expense of His own Son, Jesus Christ. Why does He offer to do such a thing for us? Why did Henry Moorehouse choose to help a little girl who had nothing to offer him in return? One word: grace. God's unwarranted burst of generosity.

The apostle Paul described this grace in Ephesians 2:4-5:

> But God, being rich in mercy, because of His great love with which
> He loved us, even when we were dead in our transgressions, made
> us alive together with Christ (by grace you have been saved).

I wonder how that little girl treated her new pitcher the next morning when she went to fill it with milk. Do you suppose she carelessly tossed it in the air as she made her way to market or balanced it on her head, thinking, *If it shatters, no big deal. That nice man will give me another one*? I doubt it. I imagine she treasured that pitcher, carefully guarding the gift that had been freely and unexpectedly purchased for her.

Grace...It Really Is Amazing

Grace is an amazing gift—no doubt about it. But it is a gift that is subject to abuse either by those who would deny its existence or by those who would distort its meaning.

In 1990 Chuck Swindoll wrote a landmark book titled *The Grace Awakening* in which he challenged Christians to reclaim the biblical doctrine of grace.[2] Chuck reminded us that we are surrounded by "grace killers," people who are still trying to earn God's favor by keeping some custom-made list of rules and regulations. Thirty or forty years ago, such a list might have included no dancing, no drinking, and no movies on Sunday. Today the list might include no public schools, no divorce and remarriage under any circumstances, and no Harry Potter novels. Since the days of Jesus and the apostle Paul, religious people have been trying to impose their opinions and prejudices on others. And the practice continues today.

I love the story Chuck tells in his book *Simple Faith* about a man who was worried about missing a flight. He wasn't wearing his watch that day and had trouble finding a clock in the terminal, so he asked a stranger for the time. The stranger pleasantly responded, "No problem," and placed his heavy suitcases on the ground beside him. Looking at his watch, the stranger announced, "The time is 5:09 precisely, it's 73 degrees outside, and we're going to get some rain tonight. Weather in London is clear at 38 degrees Celsius with a falling barometric pressure of 29.14. It's also bright and sunny in Singapore."

"Is that what your watch says?" asked the man.

"Yes, and it tells me a great deal more. It's my own invention, the only one of its kind in the world."

When he heard this, the man offered to buy the watch from the stranger for two thousand dollars.

The stranger replied that the watch wasn't for sale and began to gather his luggage to leave.

But the man persisted. "How about four thousand dollars in cash right now?" he urged, pulling out his wallet.

The stranger again declined, telling the man that he had made the watch especially for his son and intended to give it to him on his twenty-first birthday.

This time the man offered him ten thousand dollars on the spot.

"For an offer like that, I'll gladly sell you this watch," said the stranger.

Beside himself with joy, the man handed over the money and imme-diately strapped the watch on his wrist. Then he thanked the stranger and began to walk away.

But the stranger called after him, "Wait!" Then smiling broadly, he gave the man the two large suitcases he had been carrying and said, "You need the *batteries*."[3]

Legalists are those who weigh us down with a lot of extra baggage. To the new Christian who has just discovered God's grace, they cry, "Wait! Here are some additional things you need to do to earn God's forgiveness." To the seasoned believer, these grace killers scream, "Wait! The Bible alone is not sufficient to show you how to live. Here are some additional guide-lines you need to follow," and we are handed luggage filled with opinions and prejudices disguised as "truth," "obedience," or "spiritual maturity."

That's why I'm grateful for books like Swindoll's *The Grace Awakening,* Philip Yancey's *What's So Amazing About Grace?* Max Lucado's *In the Grip of Grace,* and many other fine volumes that remind us that grace means there is nothing we can do to cause God to love us any more than He already does.

However, I fear that the pendulum has swung too far in the other direction, as is so often the case.

The Dark Side of Grace

In an attempt to "rescue" grace from legalists, we have unwittingly deliv-ered it into the hands of libertarians, who insist that grace exempts Chris-tians from any standard of conduct. Instead of saying that there is nothing we need to do to cause God to love us any more than He already does, a libertarian places the period after the word *do.* "Grace means there is noth-ing we need to do."

In several of my previous books, I have attempted to answer these questions: Why is there so little difference between the lifestyles of Christians and non-Christians? Why are believers just as likely as unbelievers to fall into immorality, divorce their mates, refuse to forgive others, cheat on their taxes, and inflate their expense accounts? In *The Solomon Secrets,* I said that many Christians simply do not possess the *skill* (which Proverbs calls "wisdom") necessary to live distinctively. In *I Want More!* I pointed out that some Christians lack the *spiritual resources* necessary to live distinctively. Although every Christian experiences the *presence* of the Holy Spirit, few Christians experience the *power* of the Holy Spirit necessary for supernatural living.

But I am convinced that a foundational reason most Christians are not living more obediently is because they don't realize that they are supposed to! Oh sure, we all know God would like us to be faithful to our mates, give sacrificially to His work, forgive our offenders, be honest in our business dealings, and place His interests above our own. But if we fail, no big deal! After all, we are under grace.

Such an attitude reminds me of a young man who was confronted by a fellow Christian about cheating on his wife. When asked what he thought God's attitude toward his infidelity was, he responded, "Well, of course, I expect God to forgive me—that's His job!"[4]

Those who abuse the gift of grace focus on God's "job" of forgiving, but they have very little to say about our responsibility to obey. In fact, any attempt to remind Christians of God's standards for marriage, morality, financial stewardship, evangelism, or any other area of life is branded as "legalism." Is it any wonder, then, that there is so little difference between the lifestyles of Christians and non-Christians?

While it is true that there is nothing we can do to earn God's love, there are plenty of things we must do to enjoy God's blessings. That is not legalism; it is obedience! The New Testament continually reminds us that living under grace does not *relieve* us of the obligation of obedience; it *intensifies* that obligation:

He who believes in the Son has eternal life; but he who does not obey the Son will not see life, but the wrath of God abides on him. (John 3:36)

He who has My commandments and keeps them is the one who loves Me; and he who loves Me will be loved by My Father, and I will love him and will disclose Myself to him. (John 14:21)

What shall we say then? Are we to continue in sin so that grace may increase? May it never be! How shall we who died to sin still live in it? (Romans 6:1-2)

The one who says, "I have come to know Him," and does not keep His commandments, is a liar, and the truth is not in him; but whoever keeps His word, in him the love of God has truly been perfected. (1 John 2:4-5)

The book you hold in your hands is an attempt to rescue the biblical doctrine of grace from both legalists who deny grace *and* libertarians who pervert grace. The first section of this book is devoted to regaining a biblical understanding of grace. In the next chapter we are going to distinguish *good grace* from *bad grace.* In Romans 6, Paul explains that living under grace does not mean that we serve *no* master (bad grace), but that we serve a *new* master (good grace).

In the third chapter we will discuss the difference between legalism and obedience. Living under grace does not mean that we are under no law (bad grace), but that we are under a new law (good grace). Contrary to popular belief, grace increases rather than lessens our obligation to an even higher standard of obedience than the law demands—a standard that leads to joy, not misery.

In the second section of the book, we will discover how good grace impacts our own decision-making process as well as our relationship with God and with others. Here are some of the questions we will consider:

- Does grace require me to hang a Kick Me sign around my neck and endure endless abuse from others?
- When does grace allow for divorce, and when does obedience require staying in a difficult marriage?
- Does grace always require me to overlook the faults of others? When does grace require that I forgive others, and when does love demand that I confront them?
- Once saved, do Christians need to ask God's forgiveness for their sins?
- How can believers in the church maintain a balance between dispensing grace and, at the same time, being "holy" and "spotless" as the Bible commands?
- When do I exercise my freedom under grace, and when do I restrict it for the benefit of others? Does the "weaker brother" principle demand that I always allow the whims of others to dictate my behavior?

In the final chapter of the book we will discover how to live under good grace by avoiding the extremes of both legalism and libertarianism.

When I first proposed this project to my publisher, everyone was enthusiastic about the need for such a book. But my insightful editor (how's that for schmoozing?) offered this suggestion: "Robert, make sure this book does not come across as an 'ear-cleaning.'" I asked for a little clarification. "People understand they need to have their ears cleaned periodically," he said, "but no one enjoys it. And they sure don't want to pay to have it done." I got the point.

Perhaps you are afraid that you have just invested your hard-earned cash to have someone snatch away God's marvelous gift of grace with one hand and, with the other hand, give you a list of endless demands for pleasing God. While such a fear is understandable, it is also predicated on a lie that the Enemy has been whispering in our ears since the beginning of time: "Obedience to God leads to misery."

We assume that the freedom to do what we want (bad grace) leads to happiness, while the responsibility to obey God (good grace) leads to unhappiness. Deep down we have the sneaking suspicion that God's reasons for giving us behavioral boundaries are more for His benefit than ours.

The other night I was flipping through some old photographs and found one taken many years ago of our family on top of Pikes Peak in Colorado. I remember that day very well. After a harrowing drive up the narrow, winding road that lacked any guardrails, we arrived at the top of the mountain. We stood there transfixed by the scenic beauty.

Suddenly, without any warning, my five-year-old daughter started running toward the edge, which also lacked any barrier. In unison my wife, Amy, and I yelled, "Stop!" Were we attempting to spoil Julia's fun? Were we depriving her of some wonderful experience in order to rob her of happiness and satisfaction? No, we were trying to prevent her from going over the cliff! Our attempt to restrict her "freedom" was primarily for her benefit, not ours. And her willingness to obey resulted in life, not death.

That, in a nutshell, is the difference between good grace and bad grace.

Good grace recognizes that behavioral boundaries exist for our benefit, not our detriment.

Bad grace removes all barriers and standards of behavior.

Good grace recognizes that we should establish boundaries for other people's behavior toward us.

Bad grace demands that we be willing to endure unlimited abuse from others.

Good grace will always motivate the child of God to cling as closely to his or her heavenly Father as possible.

Bad grace will encourage the child of God to live as close to the edge of disobedience as possible.

Good grace leads to life.

Bad grace leads to death.

CHAPTER TWO

Under New Management

John Newton understood the difference between good grace and bad grace. Newton was born on July 24, 1725, in London, England. His father commanded a merchant ship that sailed the Mediterranean Sea. Like his father, Newton had saltwater in his veins and would spend the majority of his life on the open seas. At nineteen years of age, he was enlisted to serve on the HMS *Harwich,* a British warship. Finding conditions on the ship unbearable, Newton deserted. When he was recaptured shortly afterward, he was flogged in front of his shipmates for his disobedience. Newton then requested to be transferred to a slave ship and was eventually granted his request. On this new ship, he served the slave trader, who abused him so terribly that he would have died had he not been rescued by a sea captain who was a friend of Newton's father.

In time Newton would command his own slave ship, and, ironically, he subjected his slaves to the same abuses he had endured. Newton's mother, who died when he was a child, had attempted to impart her Christian convictions to him, but her efforts seemed to have been wasted on him. Newton had no use for religion. However, on May 10, 1748, everything changed.

Newton was sailing his ship home when he encountered a violent storm. Convinced that this storm would result in his death, he cried out for help, "Lord, have mercy upon us!" Once the storm had passed, Newton sat in his cabin and reflected on what he had just experienced. From that moment on, Newton observed that day of his "great deliverance" as the moment when God spoke to him in the midst of the storm and grace began to work in his life.

Although Newton would continue to command a slave ship for several years after his conversion, he became well known for treating his slaves humanely. In 1755 Newton gave up sailing and moved to Liverpool where he worked as a surveyor of tides. There he became a disciple of the great evangelist George Whitefield and an admirer of John Wesley. Hungry to know the Word of God more deeply, he taught himself Greek and Hebrew. Eventually, Newton was ordained and became pastor of a church in Olney, England. It was during those years of ministry in Olney that Newton wrote what is perhaps the most familiar and beloved song in the history of the church:

Amazing grace! how sweet the sound
That saved a wretch like me!
I once was lost, but now am found,
Was blind, but now I see.

'Twas grace that taught my heart to fear,
And grace my fears relieved
How precious did that grace appear,
The hour I first believed!

Through many dangers, toils and snares
I have already come;
'Tis grace that brought me safe thus far,
And grace will lead me home.[1]

Several years ago, I had the opportunity to preach in Olney, England. Standing in the pulpit where Newton had once proclaimed God's amazing grace to crowds so large that the church had to be expanded was an experience I will never forget. But what made an even more indelible impression on me was reading the epitaph on Newton's gravestone in the little church cemetery:

John Newton, Clerk, once an infidel and libertine, a servant of slaves in Africa, was by the rich mercy of our Lord and Saviour Jesus Christ, preserved, restored, pardoned, and appointed to preach the faith he had long labored to destroy.

In an instant John Newton had been transformed from a trader of slaves to a slave of Jesus Christ, "appointed to preach the faith." Grace did not free him to serve *no* master; instead, it freed him to serve a *new* master.

Those of us who don't have dramatic conversion stories like John Newton's may sometimes feel as though we have a second-class faith. I remember as a teenager sitting in a Sunday-evening discipleship class at church, listening as one student tried to top another in relating the sordid details of his life before coming to Christ.

Finally the leader called on me to share my story. I walked slowly to the podium and in an unusually quiet and somber tone, I began: "My parents were both addicted to hard drugs. So I began experimenting with drugs myself. It wasn't long until I was shooting up heroin three times a day. Numerous visits to detox units could not break the stranglehold that drugs had on my life.

"One night a group of friends persuaded me to join them in robbing a local 7-Eleven. My job was to point the gun at the clerk while my friends stuffed the cash from the register into their bags. I didn't mean for the gun to discharge, but somehow it did, and the clerk fell to the ground."

By this time, the only thing you could hear in the room were the muted sobs of some of the hormonally supercharged teenage girls at the back of the room who had no idea of my horrible past. I paused dramatically and delivered the punch line of my testimony: "Then…I turned five years of age and trusted in Christ as my Savior."

The stunned silence in the room was replaced by raucous laughter when everyone realized they'd been "had." (Well, everyone was laughing except the leader.) Thirty-five years later, people who were there still remind me of the night I shared my "testimony."

If you trusted in Christ at an early age, as I did, perhaps you long for a more dramatic conversion story. You may be wishing that you could share how God delivered you from a life of debauchery in a dramatic Damascus Road experience. But for many of us, stealing another child's crayons in preschool is about the worst form of corruption we can recount. It is difficult to report any real, measurable change that has occurred in our lives since we came to Christ.

But in reality, every experience of grace, regardless of the circumstances, is a radical experience that results in revolutionary changes. Let's allow the apostle Paul to be our guide as we examine the seven radical changes that God's grace brings into our lives. In this chapter we'll discuss five of these changes, and we'll cover the final two changes in the following chapter.

A New Awareness

We have sung Newton's "Amazing Grace" so many times that many of us have become numb to the words. For example, have you ever stopped to consider the paradox of the first two lines of the second stanza?

'Twas grace that taught my heart to fear,
And grace my fears relieved.

How can grace inculcate fear and at the same time relieve fear? And why would we ever desire a grace that taught us to fear in the first place? Isn't fear something to be avoided at all costs?

Perhaps this illustration will help. Approximately one baby in four hundred thousand is born with familial dysautonomia. If you are as unfamiliar with that diagnosis as I was, it simply means that the child is unable to feel pain. "What's wrong with that?" you might ask. "Wouldn't we all like to live in a pain-free world?"

But without pain, these children have no idea that they've cut or burned themselves or even that they've broken a bone. They will never complain to their parents about feeling sick, so the parents are often unaware that anything is wrong—until it's too late.[2] Pain is God's "gift" that alerts us to our need for healing.

Similarly, we must be able to experience spiritual pain over the disease of sin that is destroying our lives before we will ever be motivated to accept God's remedy for our sickness. Unfortunately, without the gift of grace, our spiritual nerve endings are dead, unable to sense our spiritual condition. The apostle Paul describes our condition this way:

> You were dead in your trespasses and sins, in which you formerly
> walked according to the course of this world, according to the
> prince of the power of the air, of the spirit that is now working
> in the sons of disobedience. (Ephesians 2:1-2)

We tend to undervalue the magnitude of God's grace when we underestimate our desperate situation prior to our coming to Christ. Some people believe that we are born slightly flawed but basically good. Given the right environment and circumstances, we will be just fine. Others believe—including many Christians—that people apart from Christ are basically bad. We have inherited a seriously defective nature from Adam that pulls us away from God. However, there is just enough of God's image left in us that, given the opportunity, we can choose to follow God.

But Paul says that apart from the grace of God we are not just slightly dented or even seriously defective. We are *dead!* A corpse has no awareness of pleasure or pain. It is completely unaware that it is trapped in a box six feet underground. It has no sense that it is rotting away. It knows nothing and feels nothing because it is dead.

To illustrate that point to my congregation, I took a video crew out to a local cemetery. As I stood on top of one of the graves, I described the following scenario to the congregation. "Imagine that you have stopped here to read the inscription on a gravestone when you see a hand thrusting up through the dirt. You are so startled you stop to see what else might happen. Soon another hand pops out, then a head, and before long a guy dressed in a suit pulls himself out of the grave. He brushes all the grass and dirt off himself and says to you, 'Boy, that sure was unpleasant. I'm glad I'm out of there!' "[3]

You might be thinking this is a ridiculous illustration. After all, dead people can't resurrect themselves! And that is exactly Paul's point in Ephesians 2. Apart from the power of Jesus Christ, every person in this world is spiritually dead, incapable of making any kind of response to God. As unbelievers we could never lift ourselves out of the grave of sin and death and suddenly choose to become Christians. We were spiritually dead, Paul says, and therefore had no awareness of our condition. Only by God's grace do we who are spiritually dead become aware of our corrupt state.

One of the benefits of grace is a painful awareness of our sin—an awareness that does not stop the moment we accept God's sin remedy. In fact, the closer we move toward God, the more aware we become of our sin. That was certainly Paul's experience. Read his lament slowly and carefully and see if you can identify with his experience:

I know that nothing good dwells in me, that is, in my flesh; for the
willing is present in me, but the doing of the good is not. For the
good that I want, I do not do, but I practice the very evil that I do
not want. But if I am doing the very thing I do not want, I am no
longer the one doing it, but sin which dwells in me.... Wretched
man that I am! Who will set me free from the body of this death?
(Romans 7:18-20,24)

Paul wrote these words *after* his conversion experience, not before.
They reflect the spiritual anguish of a Christian who is increasingly aware
of those things in his life that are displeasing to God.

Advocates of bad grace might offer this counsel to the conflicted apostle:
"Quit worrying about your sins, Paul. After all, they've been covered by the
blood of Christ. Satan is just trying to put you on a guilt trip." These folks
believe that any awareness of sin is to be avoided at all costs. Terms such as
confession, repentance, and *self-examination* should be reserved for unbelievers. Once we have received God's forgiveness, we don't need to wallow in
our mistakes, past or present. Instead, we need to press on.

But those who understand good grace realize that an awareness of sin
is not only necessary for our salvation; it is crucial for our continued spiritual health. Admittedly, when I accidentally touch a hot stove, "Praise the
Lord!" is not usually the first phrase to fall from my lips. But it should be.
The nerve endings in my finger that scream, "Stop that, you idiot!" are a
gift from our Creator to keep me from seriously injuring myself.

Similarly, the pain that disobedience brings into our lives is not to be
ignored, but welcomed as another evidence of God's grace. Without such
pain we are doomed to continue on a path that will lead to our eventual
destruction. The psalmist expressed his gratitude for the gift of spiritual
pain when he wrote, "Before I was afflicted I went astray, but now I keep
Your word" (Psalm 119:67).

The psalmist thanked God for his new awareness of sin that grace brought into his life, and so should we.

A NEW STATUS

Good grace also recognizes the radical change that has occurred in our status with God. Paul described that change in status with two striking contrasts. First, God's grace has transformed us from being God's enemy to being His friend:

> God demonstrates His own love toward us, in that while we were
> yet sinners, Christ died for us.... For if while we were enemies we
> were reconciled to God through the death of His Son, much more,
> having been reconciled, we shall be saved by His life. (Romans
> 5:8,10)

If you have hung around evangelical churches for any period of time, you have probably heard the following illustration of grace. We preacher-types love this story for both its illustrative value and its emotional impact.

A little girl was dying and desperately needed a blood transfusion. Because of her rare blood type and the urgency of her condition, the only person capable of providing the necessary blood was her little brother. The parents explained the situation to the boy, and he agreed to donate his blood.

After the transfusion was complete, the physician patted the boy's shoulder, commending him for his bravery. After a few moments of silence, the boy looked up at the doctor and inquired, "How long before I die?"

The little boy mistakenly assumed that his donation would lead to his death, a sacrifice he had been more than willing to make for his sister.

It's a sweet story, but it doesn't carry quite the punch of Paul's analogy.

It is not that unusual for a family member to be willing to die for another family member. But now let's change the story a little.

Instead of a little girl, a prisoner on death row is dying of a defective heart. Only a transplant can save his life. A man offers to donate his heart to the prisoner, but it will mean certain death for the donor. And who is the person willing to make the ultimate sacrifice? The father of a little girl the prisoner brutally murdered. Now *that* is genuine love—the kind of love God demonstrated toward us.

Apart from Christ, we are enemies of God, not His children. As one commentator writes, we are so opposed to God that we would drag Him off his throne and destroy Him if we possibly could.[4] But in the ultimate demonstration of extraordinary grace, God offered His Son as the human sacrifice for our sins so that we might receive new hearts. We who were God's enemies have now become His friends.

Paul used another contrast to illustrate the change in our status that results from God's grace. Instead of being God's slaves, we have become His sons: "Therefore you are no longer a slave, but a son; and if a son, then an heir through God" (Galatians 4:7).

In Paul's day slaves lived with the families they served and were considered a part of the household (which is why Paul included them in Ephesians 5–6 when discussing the responsibilities of husbands and wives, children and parents, and slaves and masters). But even though slaves lived in the same house as the family they served, they had no rights. And they certainly had no claim to the family's wealth.

But a son enjoyed a completely different relationship with the father of the household. He could approach his father confidently, not timidly, about any matter he chose. When the son reached a certain age (usually between fourteen and seventeen), the father bestowed on him the full rights of an adult. Furthermore, all the riches possessed by the father now belonged to the son.

This background information helps us appreciate even more Paul's analogy in Galatians 4:

> When the fullness of the time came, God sent forth His Son, born
> of a woman, born under the Law, so that He might redeem those
> who were under the Law, that we might receive the adoption as sons.
> Because you are sons, God has sent forth the Spirit of His Son into
> our hearts, crying, "Abba! Father!" Therefore you are no longer a
> slave, but a son; and if a son, then an heir through God. (verses 4-7)

The Bible uses two metaphors to describe how we enter God's family. Sometimes our entrance into the family of God is described as a new birth, as in John 3 and 1 Peter 1:3. This metaphor emphasizes the new life that has been imparted to those of us who were spiritually dead.

Other times, as in Galatians 4, our placement in God's family is described as an adoption. The Greek word for "adopt" means "to place as a son." In Paul's day it was common for wealthy couples who were childless to adopt a young adult male who could carry on the family name. The adopted son entered the family not as a child who possessed few rights but as an adult who possessed full rights as an heir to the family fortune.

In Galatians 4, Paul explained that when we become part of God's family through faith in Christ, our status changes, not from slaves who have no rights to children who have a *few* rights, but from slaves who have no rights to adults who have *full* rights.

A New Heart

From the days of the Old Testament, God promised His people that one day He would give them a new heart so that their obedience would not be motivated by fear but would instead be generated by desire:

Moreover, I will give you a new heart and put a new spirit within
you; and I will remove the heart of stone from your flesh and give
you a heart of flesh. I will put My Spirit within you and cause you
to walk in My statutes, and you will be careful to observe My ordi-
nances. (Ezekiel 36:26-27)

The fulfillment of that promise came after the death of Christ, which
initiated the new covenant (or agreement) between God and humans.
Shortly after Christ's death, believers received the indwelling of the Holy
Spirit prophesied in Ezekiel. And with the Holy Spirit came a brand-new
heart or nature that would strive to please God.

The only way to fully appreciate this new heart we have received is to
understand the defectiveness of our old heart (or "flesh," as Paul called it),
which we still retain:

For the flesh sets its desire against the Spirit, and the Spirit against
the flesh; for these are in opposition to one another, so that you may
not do the things that you please.... Now the deeds of the flesh are
evident, which are: immorality, impurity, sensuality, idolatry, sorcery,
enmities, strife, jealousy, outbursts of anger, disputes, dissensions,
factions. (Galatians 5:17,19-20)

Do you ever struggle with impure thoughts? Do you find yourself
thinking about and loving other people or things more than you love God?
Do you sometimes have difficulty controlling your temper? If you found
out that God didn't exist, what would you start doing that you aren't doing
now out of fear of Him? Don't be pious; be honest.

Congratulations! Your answers reveal that you're human, which is another
way of saying that you still have the remains of the defective heart you were
born with, thanks to your great, great, great, great-grandfather Adam.

But let's not stop there. Do you sometimes long to know God better? Do you feel a sense of satisfaction when you have an opportunity to share the gospel with another person? Is something stirred in your innermost being when you are involved in worship? Congratulations again! You are the recipient of a new heart as well.

So what is the relationship between our old heart and our new heart? To repeat a popular phrase, it's a dysfunctional relationship. Or, as Paul said, they "are in opposition to one another" (Galatians 5:17).

Years ago Steve Martin starred in the movie comedy *The Man with Two Brains.* Martin hilariously portrayed the internal conflict of a man who was being governed by two opposing forces that were constantly battling each other.

But for the apostle Paul, such a phenomenon was no laughing matter. As he experienced personally, the part of him that wanted to please God waged war against the part of him that didn't:

> It seems to be a fact of life that when I want to do what is right, I inevitably do what is wrong. I love God's law with all my heart. But there is another law at work within me that is at war with my mind. This law wins the fight and makes me a slave to the sin that is still within me. Oh, what a miserable person I am! Who will free me from this life that is dominated by sin? (Romans 7:21-24, NLT)

Paul believed that even though such a war of the wills is inevitable, it is also possible to win that war. Why? Because, contrary to popular belief, our two hearts are not equally powerful. In fact, Paul says that when we became Christians, our old heart or "self" was "crucified with Him, in order that our body of sin might be done away with, so that we would no longer be slaves to sin; for he who has died is freed from sin" (Romans 6:6-7).

But what exactly does that mean? For years the idea of my old heart being crucified made absolutely no sense to me because it was contrary to my daily (make that hourly) experience. My old nature was alive and well and enjoying regular victories, so how could it be dead? Let me illustrate how something can be defeated yet still be active.

For many years the nation of Iraq suffered under the brutal dictatorship of Saddam Hussein. The majority of people had no freedom and lived in constant fear of Hussein and his henchmen. Then on March 19, 2003, America invaded Iraq and quickly defeated Hussein's regime in an amazing display of military might. The entire world marveled at the United States' power in winning such a decisive victory in so brief a period of time. Many residents of Iraq cheered their liberation from a tyrannical ruler. The U.S. military set up command posts in the heart of the country to protect the citizens as they began to rebuild their nation.

But our occupation of Iraq did not end the enemy attacks. Even though America had won the war, guerrilla forces sympathetic to Saddam Hussein continued to ambush both the American troops and Iraqi citizens. No one doubted the reality of America's liberation of Iraq, but that victory did not exempt citizens and occupying forces from daily enemy assaults.

Similarly, Jesus Christ won a decisive victory over sin at the cross more than two thousand years ago. At that moment our Savior liberated all of us who trust in Him from the brutal regime of Satan. The Holy Spirit has set up a command post in the heart of every Christian. Although we are still subject to guerrilla attacks by the Enemy, we possess the necessary firepower to win those battles. In fact, we have as much ability to prevail in those skirmishes as a nuclear superpower has to overcome a scraggly rebel soldier toting nothing more than a .45-caliber pistol.

What does all this have to do with good grace and bad grace? A faulty understanding of grace tends to overemphasize the power of our old heart and underemphasize the potency of our new one. Because of the occasional attacks by some of the Enemy's renegade forces, bad grace wrongly assumes that we are still under Satan's control. Whatever desire we have to break free from his grip is not powerful enough to deliver us from such a formidable foe. The result is a resigned acquiescence—if not a resolute acceptance—of sin as a way of life.

No! Paul screams from the pages of his letter to the Romans. The war was already fought—and won—two thousand years ago on the battlefield called Calvary. You are free from Satan's dictatorship—now live like it!

A New Master

You've probably heard this question before or perhaps even voiced it yourself: "If God's grace means that I am completely forgiven of all my sins—past, present, and future—what is to keep me from sinning as much as I want?" Such a question fails to take into account the new heart we discussed in the last section that changes the "as much as I want" part of the question. Our new heart radically transforms our desire to serve Satan and his interests into a desire to serve God and His interests.

But this question contains another faulty premise that characterizes bad grace: the assumption that grace frees us to do whatever we want. In truth, grace frees us not to serve *no* master but to serve a *new* master. The apostle Paul was regularly accused of promoting bad grace by the legalists of his day. "Paul, if you teach that obedience to the Law will not save us, aren't you encouraging us to disobey the Law?" Paul denied the accusation in the strongest possible way:

What then? Shall we sin because we are not under law but under grace? May it never be! (Romans 6:15)

He then exposed the flawed assumption underlying such an assertion by pointing out a very unpopular fact:

Do you not know that when you present yourselves to someone as slaves for obedience, you are slaves of the one whom you obey, either of sin resulting in death, or of obedience resulting in righteousness? (verse 16)

Paul was saying, "I have some good news and some bad news for you. The bad news is that we are all slaves to something. None of us is free. We are in bondage to whatever controls our lives." Or as the apostle Peter put it, "You are a slave to whatever controls you" (2 Peter 2:19, NLT). The person who can't say no to sweets is a slave to sugar. The Christian who cannot turn off the television to read the Bible or spend time with his or her children is a slave to the tube. The man (or woman) who cannot break an addiction to pornography is a slave to immorality. The person who checks his or her stock portfolio on CNBC every hour is a slave to money. We are slaves to whatever controls our lives. Jesus inferred the same truth when He declared,

No one can serve two masters; for either he will hate the one and love the other, or he will be devoted to one and despise the other. (Matthew 6:24)

No one can serve two masters—but everyone serves *one* master. That's the bad news.

But here's the good news: We get to choose our master. As we saw in the previous section, a non-Christian has no choice of masters. He is a slave to his old nature and therefore a slave to Satan. As hard as he may try to break free, the chains of sin keep yanking him back. He can never break free. He is Satan's indentured servant.

But a Christian has been liberated to serve a new Master. Paul explained it this way:

Thanks be to God that though you were slaves of sin, you became obedient from the heart to that form of teaching to which you were committed, and having been freed from sin, you became slaves of righteousness. (Romans 6:17-18)

Paul later equated being "slaves of righteousness" with being "slaves of God" (Romans 6:22, NLT). As we will see in the next chapter, being "enslaved to God" is not as miserable as it sounds. The "wages" we receive from serving Him are much more lucrative than anything Satan has ever offered us.

So why do Christians still sin? Because we occasionally choose to serve our old master rather than our new one, even though our previous slave master has no authority over our lives. The following scenario illustrates the absurdity of that choice:

Imagine that you are living in an apartment house under a landlord who has made your life miserable. He charges an astronomically high rent, and when you are unable to pay, he tacks on exorbitant interest that only gets you further in debt. He barges into your apartment at all hours, breathing threats, soiling your carpet, and then charging you extra for not maintaining the property!

One day you open your door and find a stranger standing there. "I'm the new owner of this apartment building. I'm sorry for all you have experienced under the previous owner, but I want you to know you can live here—for free—as long as you want." You are elated over the change in management. Finally, you have been delivered from the clutches of the previous owner.

Then one day there is a loud knocking at the door. There is your old landlord cursing loudly and demanding you pay him the overdue rent. How should you respond? Would you pay him what he demands? Of course not! He is no longer the owner of the building. Would you attack him? Probably not, especially if he is bigger than you are. Instead, you would explain to him that he no longer has any authority over you since your apartment is now under new management. If he has a complaint, he can take it up with the new owner.

The old landlord may continue to bluster and threaten you, hoping he can bluff you into paying him, but he knows he has no real authority over you. He is just hoping you don't know that.[5]

A New Location

Practitioners of bad grace also fail to recognize the radical change of location for Christians. Paul describes our new "address" this way:

> God, being rich in mercy, because of His great love with which He loved us, even when we were dead in our transgressions, made us alive together with Christ (by grace you have been saved), and raised us up with Him, and seated us *with Him in the heavenly places* in Christ Jesus. (Ephesians 2:4-6)

The phrase "He raised us up" refers not to the resurrection of Jesus (Paul alluded to that in verse 5) but to His ascension. At the Ascension (Acts 1:6-11) God lifted Jesus out of this world into an entirely different world. In the same way, those of us who follow Christ have been lifted out of the graveyard of sin into an entirely different realm of living. Why would we ever choose to return to our old way of life?

Remember the story of Lazarus? When news of his death reached Jesus, the Lord traveled to Bethany to perform His greatest miracle of all time.

Standing in front of the sepulcher where His friend had been buried four days earlier, Jesus ordered the stone removed in the presence of Lazarus's sisters and friends.

> [Jesus] cried out with a loud voice, "Lazarus, come forth." The man
> who had died came forth, bound hand and foot with wrappings,
> and his face was wrapped around with a cloth. Jesus said to them,
> "Unbind him, and let him go." (John 11:43-44)

In the days before embalming, a corpse was wrapped in one hundred pounds of spices and cloth to preserve the body from premature decay. Obviously, now that Lazarus was alive, he had no need for these wrappings. So the Lord ordered, "Unbind him, and let him go" (verse 44).

Do you think Lazarus protested when he heard Jesus's command, saying, "Lord, I've grown rather fond of these wrappings. Please don't make me take them off!"? Or can you fathom Lazarus saying, "Come out? I like it here in the sepulcher. It's quiet and cool." Do you suppose that once Jesus left, Lazarus secretly returned to the tomb at night, covered himself in those cloths and spices, and lay back down?

Such a thought is preposterous! Graveclothes are suitable only for the dead, not for the living. The only people who feel comfortable setting up residence in a cemetery are those who have died, not those who are alive!

Again, you may wonder what this has to do with good grace and bad grace. People with a defective view of grace assume that those who have experienced God's forgiveness would still prefer to live in sin rather than live in obedience to God. While it's true that we are free to live in sin, why would we want to? Or, as Paul asked, "How shall we who died to sin still live in it?" (Romans 6:2).

For you and me to choose to sin makes about as much sense as choosing to crawl into a grave while we are still alive. For us to get wrapped up in immorality, greed, gossip, and bitterness is about as logical as Lazarus choosing to clothe himself again with those foul-smelling graveclothes. We can do it, but why would we ever want to?

CHAPTER THREE

Laying Down the Law...
Without Giving Up Grace

I have loved James Bond movies since I was a little boy. Before you send me any letters of protest over the violence and immorality that fill this popular series of spy flicks, you should know that my affection for James Bond is my mom's fault. When I was ten years old, my mother was scheduled to attend an all-day teachers' conference at Texas Christian University in Fort Worth. Not having the money to hire a baby-sitter, she dropped me off at a theater right across the street from the TCU campus and told me she would pick me up when her meeting was over. That meant that I sat through four complete showings of *Thunderball*. To this day I can recite entire passages from that movie! Thus began my love affair with Secret Agent 007.

Those of you who are at all familiar with Bond (remember this is a book about grace, so you don't have to live in shame), know that the 00 designation refers to a special class of agents on Her Majesty's Secret Service who possess what ordinary spies don't—and I'm not referring to beautiful babes and fast cars. This group of agents has been given a license to kill. They never have to secure permission or offer explanations for taking another person's life. The 00 designation means they are above the law that normal citizens live by.

Unfortunately, many Christians today live under the delusion that as recipients of God's forgiveness and participants in His Majesty's service, they, too, possess a special privilege: a license to sin. Whenever a spiritual policeman (a pastor, family member, or fellow Christian) confronts them about the issue of obedience, they simply flash their special license, which is spelled G-R-A-C-E.

I recently learned about a well-known Christian who was confronted by a group of concerned friends about an adulterous affair he was having. His response? He whipped out his "license" and said, "I am living under grace, not law."

As we saw in the last chapter, such a response betrays a defective view of grace. God's grace is not a license to do what we want, but the liberty to do what we should. Anyone who uses grace as a cover for sin does not understand the seven radical changes that grace produces in the life of a genuine believer. In chapter 2 we looked at five of those changes, and in this chapter we will examine two more.

In spite of the new awareness, status, nature, Master, and location that grace provides us, we all periodically succumb to the threats of our old "landlord" and give in to his demands. So what is the answer to our sin dilemma? The proponents of bad grace go to one of two extremes in addressing the sin problem with which we all wrestle.

PHARISEES ARE ALIVE AND WELL...AND IN YOUR CHURCH

One extreme is legalism. A legalist underestimates the power of our new nature to motivate us to obey God and therefore feels compelled to close up any loopholes in God's Word that might allow believers to escape their duty to obey. Years ago when I was being interviewed by the pastoral-search committee of a particular church, one of the committee members wanted to know my position on divorce and remarriage. I replied that although God hates divorce, He does allow for divorce and remarriage in two specific circumstances. (I will discuss these circumstances in chapter 8.)

Amazingly, the committee member disagreed not with my interpretation of Scripture but with my desire to adhere exclusively to the Scriptures. "If you give Christians the freedom to divorce under those circumstances, everyone will find a way out of their marriage vows," he insisted. Relying on our new nature and the new standard of conduct revealed in Scripture is not sufficient for the legalist who insists on additional rules beyond the Bible to make sure that everyone stays in line.

Here is a simple definition of legalism: obedience to the wrong standard for the wrong reasons. Legalists constantly add to the Bible's standards of conduct for Christians. They tend to place Christians under a code of conduct that is either based on antiquated Jewish laws that are not applicable to Christians today or on the opinions and prejudices of others.

Dr. Richard Mayhue notes some of the more common rules that legalists advocate:

1. "Specifying the only authorized version of the English Bible." (Some churches insist that the *King James Version* is the only acceptable translation.)
2. "Forbidding certain kinds of entertainment." (This might include movies, dancing, and so on.)
3. "Keeping the Sabbath." (This would mean abstaining from certain activities on Sundays, such as eating out, shopping, or work.)
4. "Outlawing certain musical instruments." (Some churches ban the use of guitars and drums during worship.)
5. "Demanding one method of schooling over another." (This might mean insisting that children be homeschooled.)

6. "Imposing extra rules of conduct." (This might include forbidding the consumption of any kind of alcoholic beverage.)[1]

The last one reminds me of a story about a man in Georgia who operated a restaurant in a "dry" county. When he asked the county commissioners to grant him permission to put wine on the menu, they denied his request. The restaurant owner tried to appeal the decision on biblical grounds. "You know, even Jesus drank wine."

"That may be true," answered one of the commissioners, who was also a Baptist deacon. "And that's always embarrassed me!"[2]

Not only do legalists employ a faulty standard for conduct, they also offer an erroneous incentive for obedience to the standard they have manufactured. In its strictest sense, legalism is an attempt to earn our salvation by adherence to a code of conduct. Legalism implies that faith in Christ is necessary but not sufficient to secure God's forgiveness. Thus, when asked what a person must do to gain eternal life, a legalist answers, "You must trust in Jesus Christ *and*...be baptized, or keep the law, or confess your sins to a priest, or join this church or denomination."

While reaching the pearly gates of heaven is the primary incentive legalists use to encourage adherence to a list of requirements, it is not their only "carrot." Some legalists who concede that salvation is by grace use self-manufactured standards to achieve another goal: sanctification (the process by which we become more like Christ after we're saved). This form of bad grace employs the right incentive (who could argue with becoming more like Jesus?), but it uses the wrong standard by which to accomplish that goal.

Convinced that God's Word is not sufficient by itself to govern our conduct, those who advocate this form of legalism concoct a formula for living consisting of one part Bible, two parts personal preferences, one part tradition, and a heavy sprinkling of personal prejudice. It is a bitter brew to swallow, and a legalist is not content to drink it alone. Insisting that everyone partake of the same standard, he forces others to drink what he himself sometimes refuses to consume. (Jesus often referred to this kind of hypocrisy in his scathing criticism of the Pharisees, who were the legalists of his day.)

You might ask, "But Robert, the Bible doesn't address every decision I must make. Am I a legalist for preferring the *King James Version* over *The Living Bible*, or for choosing to homeschool my children instead of sending them to public schools, or for choosing to abstain from alcohol instead of joining my Christian friends in an occasional drink?"

Not at all! Each of us must seek and follow God's leading in these and many other issues. The legalist's error is assuming that God is going to lead everyone to make the same decision the legalist has made. A great definition of legalism is "forcing my opinion to become your conviction."

We have the right—and the obligation—to persuade others to follow the clear standards for behavior as outlined in Scripture. But in matters about which the Bible is silent, we should ask for God's guidance and allow others to do the same.

You are probably familiar with the story of Eric Liddell, the Scottish runner immortalized in the movie *Chariots of Fire* for his willingness to sacrifice a gold medal in the 1924 Paris Olympics for his conviction not to run on Sundays. Later in life Liddell served as a missionary to China and was incarcerated in a Japanese prison camp. There he refereed the children's basketball and hockey games. But out of personal conviction, he refused to officiate on Sundays. But because he wasn't there to help out on Sundays, the children quarreled with one another. Realizing that the children needed this diversion from their grim situation, Liddell changed his mind and agreed to referee on Sundays. Although he himself would never have engaged in athletics on the Lord's Day, rather than enforcing a standard of legalism on others, he extended grace.[3]

The Other Extreme

Reacting to legalism, an increasing number of Christians have embraced another mutation of bad grace that denies *any* standard of behavior for Christians. "Freedom in Christ" is the rallying cry for those who continually insist that "we live under grace, not law." Standards of morality, marriage, financial stewardship, responsibility in God's kingdom work, or any other area of life are sidestepped because they are viewed as negating God's grace. "You are trying to place me under the law" is a common objection of those who misunderstand grace to be a license to do whatever they want to do.

But the apostle Paul, who was the originator of the phrase "[we] are not under law but under grace" (Romans 6:14), had a completely different understanding of grace. In Romans 6–7, Paul carefully explained that just as grace frees us to serve a new Master instead of no master, it also places us under a new law, not under no law. Furthermore, grace provides us with a new motivation for obeying our new Master's law.

A New Law

The chief characteristic of bad grace is its natural aversion to any kind of rules. One writer describes the attitude of many proponents of bad grace:

> According to Paul, I am not under law. That has radical practical consequences for my Christian life. It means I do not have to look over my shoulder at the law and judge my life by it. The law was a negative standard. It was filled with prohibitions and punishments. Grace is the opposite. It is filled with positive inducements and promises. Which would you rather have as a rule of life? *I live*

under grace, not law. And that means whenever the law brings its negative message—when it says, "thou shalt not"—it does not apply to me.[4]

This description of bad grace demonstrates three common misunderstandings about the law. First, "bad gracers" assume that the law (a reference to the sum total of the ceremonial, civil, and moral laws recorded in the Old Testament) is evil. The apostle Paul, anticipating this reaction to his declaration that we no longer live "under law," said just the opposite:

Is the Law sin? May it never be! On the contrary, I would not have come to know sin except through the Law; for I would not have known about coveting if the Law had not said, "You shall not covet."... So then, the Law is holy, and the commandment is holy and righteous and good. (Romans 7:7,12)

Imagine that you go to your doctor complaining of chest pains. Deciding that your symptoms warrant further examination, he places you on a table as an x-ray machine slowly passes over your chest. After a few minutes he invites you into a small, darkened room where your x-ray is displayed against a lighted background. With a scowl he points to a dark spot in the center of your chest. "That is the problem. You have a tumor that must be removed immediately, or you will die."

Would you cry out, "If only I had not allowed the doctor to x-ray my chest, I would be fine!"? Obviously, the x-ray itself is not your problem; it only reveals your problem.

Similarly, Paul reasoned that the law is a spiritual x-ray that diagnoses the sin problem residing within each of us. God's law reveals the dark places in the inner recesses of our hearts and hopefully motivates us to allow the

Great Physician to remove the tumor of sin that threatens our well-being. The law is good as long as we use it correctly—or, as Paul says, "lawfully" (1 Timothy 1:8).

Speaking of doctors, I love the story about the patient whose physician tells him, "You need this operation, or you will die."

"How much will the operation cost?" the patient inquires.

The doctor answers, "Ten thousand dollars, or for five hundred dollars I'll be happy to touch up your x-ray!"

To attempt to use God's law to achieve spiritual health is just as foolish as depending on a "doctored" x-ray to improve our physical condition.

In addition to the assumption that the law is evil, a second erroneous assumption common to bad grace is the belief that Christians are under no law. You may say, "But Robert, didn't Paul declare that we are no longer under the law?" Yes, he used that phrase repeatedly, especially in his letter to the Galatians. But a closer study of Paul's words reveals that he had two specific ideas in mind when he said that Christians are no longer under the law.

First, Paul was declaring that Christians are not under the spiritual "health-care plan" that requires complete obedience to the law for salvation—an impossible requirement. Instead, we have opted for a superior plan that provides salvation by faith in Christ alone. In that sense, we are not under the law, but we are under grace.

Second, Paul used the phrase "under the law" in Galatians to refer primarily to the detailed ceremonial laws that were unique to Israel, such as circumcision and dietary restrictions. In the early days of the church, Jewish Christians—who were among the first converts and leaders in the church—were constantly arguing over the need for Gentile (non-Jewish) converts to keep the ceremonial regulations of the Old Testament.

At a council meeting in Jerusalem, church leaders determined that Gentile converts were not obligated to follow the Old Testament ceremonial laws regarding circumcision, diet, and observance of religious rituals (see Acts 15). While some of these regulations—especially the dietary ones—might result in longer and healthier life—no Christian is obligated to keep them. That is why Paul wrote to the Christians at Colossae:

> No one is to act as your judge in regard to food or drink or in re-
> spect to a festival or a new moon or a Sabbath day—things which
> are a mere shadow of what is to come; but the substance belongs to
> Christ. (Colossians 2:16-17)

Although we are not under the old law, as detailed in the Old Testament, that doesn't mean we are not under *any* law.

I think about the young man who was tired of his parents' rules about curfews, grooming, and chores around the house. "I can't wait until I'm old enough to get out of here so that I can join the marines." Poor guy! He was about to trade one set of rules for a different and, in many ways, stricter set of rules.

Grace does not free us from all requirements, just from the requirements of the old law. Now that we serve a new Master, we also are obligated to follow His commands:

> Do you not know that when you present yourselves to someone as
> slaves for obedience, you are slaves of the one whom you obey,
> either of sin resulting in death, or of obedience resulting in right-
> eousness?... For just as you presented your members as slaves to
> impurity and to lawlessness, resulting in further lawlessness, so now
> present your members as slaves to righteousness, resulting in sancti-
> fication. (Romans 6:16,19)

Here's the Jeffress paraphrase of Paul's words: "You are obligated to obey the requirements of whatever master you choose to serve. If you want to be a slave to Satan, then you are obligated to obey his demands. If you want to be a slave to Jesus Christ, then you must obey His demands."

Yes, Jesus *does* place demands on those who choose to follow Him. Here are just a few of them:

A new commandment I give to you, that you love one another, even as I have loved you, that you also love one another. (John 13:34)

You have heard that it was said, "You shall not commit adultery"; but I say to you that everyone who looks at a woman with lust for her has already committed adultery with her in his heart. (Matthew 5:27-28)

Again, you have heard that the ancients were told, "You shall not make false vows, but shall fulfill your vows to the Lord." But I say to you, make no oath at all, either by heaven, for it is the throne of God, or by the earth, for it is the footstool of His feet. (Matthew 5:33-35)

I could go on, but you get the idea. Grace does not free us from all obligation to obedience; instead, it actually obligates us to a greater standard of obedience than the old law ever dreamed possible. Even Paul, the great crusader for grace, wrote about the "law of Christ" (Galatians 6:2) that governs those of us who are recipients of grace.

You might be wondering if grace really offers us any benefits if we are simply exchanging one master for a new Master and one set of requirements for a new and stricter set of requirements. Before you conclude that grace is not really that amazing, consider the new incentive for obedience that grace offers.

A New Incentive

We are slaves to whatever controls our lives. As we saw in chapter 2, non-Christians are slaves to sin. They are unable to keep from sinning. But occasionally, some non-Christians come to their senses—like the prodigal son in Luke 15—and realize what a cruel taskmaster sin is. They genuinely desire to escape Satan's brutal stranglehold on their lives. And so a new master appears, offering them freedom if they can simply pay the price for it themselves. This new master's name is "legalism," and his price for freedom is obedience to God's law. So the slaves thumb their noses at their old master and begin serving their new master, who has promised them far better lives than they have ever experienced.

However, the slaves soon find that life under their new master is not much different from life under their former one. They are still in bondage to their desires. They still suffer cruel punishment for their wrong choices. They are still fearful about what awaits them on the other side of the grave. What about all the promises the new master offered? To their horror, the slaves discover one day that their new master is an employee of their former master. They have been duped. All along they have been serving their former master.

In the Bible, both sin and legalism are compared to slavery. Those who attempt to purchase freedom from sin through legalism don't realize that their "new" master is really just one of Satan's lackeys. Our Enemy, understanding the spiritual bent we have retained even after Adam's fall, cons some of us into thinking we can buy our way out of our sin problem through selective obedience to some moral code. If we can just keep enough of God's regulations, perhaps He will grant us freedom. However, as we have seen, the purchase price for our freedom is far beyond our ability to pay.

That is why the apostle Paul compared legalism to slavery (see Galatians 4:21-31). Religious people who are attempting to earn their way to heaven through obedience to God's law are still prisoners to sin. Any occasional victory they experience over their old nature is overshadowed by more frequent defeats. Even though they are slavishly attempting to follow God's law, they are still in bondage, because their motivation for obedience is fear.

By contrast, Christians who have been set free to serve God are still obligated to follow their new Master's rules, but for a completely different reason. As slaves of Jesus Christ, our motive for obedience is our genuine desire to receive our Master's approval, not to earn our redemption.

Part of this desire originates from an inherent obligation we feel to serve the One who redeemed us. It is not popular, especially among the proponents of bad grace, to speak of our duty to obey. Some folks think that smacks of legalism. Yet the Bible does not divorce the concepts of grace and duty. Jesus vividly described the obligation His servants have to obey Him:

> Which of you, having a slave plowing or tending sheep, will say to
> him when he has come in from the field, "Come immediately and
> sit down to eat"? But will he not say to him, "Prepare something for
> me to eat, and properly clothe yourself and serve me while I eat and
> drink; and afterward you may eat and drink"? He does not thank
> the slave because he did the things which were commanded, does
> he? So you too, when you do all the things which are commanded
> you, say, "We are unworthy slaves; we have done only that which we
> ought to have done." (Luke 17:7-10)

If we denigrate obedience that is rooted in duty rather than love, we are attempting to be more spiritual than Jesus is! The Lord taught that duty is a legitimate motivation for obedience. For example, imagine going into your child's bedroom one Saturday afternoon and noticing that it is spotless. Every piece of clothing is neatly hung in the closet, the bed is made, and the wastebasket has been emptied, just as you instructed. Do you call your child in and say, "Now tell me, did you clean your room because I told you to or because you wanted to?"

And if your child answers, "Because you told me to," do you punish him or her for having the "wrong" motivation? No, you are delighted that your child respected you enough to take your commands seriously.

In the same way, our heavenly Father is pleased, not angered, when we obey Him because we respect His authority. Leroy Eims writes about a time when he was mentoring a group of young seminary students.

One of [the students] was reciting the Westminster Catechism, and the first question and answer were, "What is the chief end of man? The chief end of man is to glorify God and to enjoy him forever."

"That's great." I thought. And then I asked him, "Don, how do you glorify God? If I said to you, 'Begin glorifying God,' how would you do it?"

Don thought for a moment and then said, "I don't know. I never really thought about it."

"How are you going to glorify God if you don't know how?" I asked.

Then we did a Bible study on how to glorify God, and we focused on obedience.

How does our obedience to God glorify Him? By showing forth His authority for one thing....

When people see others obeying someone, they know that the person has authority. It is the same when people see us obeying God: they know He has authority."[5]

But in a complementary, not contradictory, passage of Scripture, Jesus also taught that our motivation for obedience goes beyond mere duty and includes our love for Him.

> If you love Me, you will keep My commandments.... Greater love has no one than this, that one lay down his life for his friends. You are My friends if you do what I command you. No longer do I call you slaves, for the slave does not know what his master is doing; but I have called you friends, for all things that I have heard from My Father I have made known to you. (John 14:15; 15:13-15)

Can duty and love coexist as motives for obedience? As I was thinking about that question, the pastor who gave me my first job in ministry came to mind—Dr. W. A. Criswell of the historic First Baptist Church in Dallas. While I was a seminary student, Dr. Criswell asked me if I would consider becoming the youth minister at his church. I eagerly accepted the offer to serve and work alongside this legendary pastor in the congregation where I had grown up.

However, Dr. Criswell had failed to ask any of the lay leaders in the youth department for their input about my hiring. Some objected, saying I was too young (which, in retrospect, I probably was). But Dr. Criswell was adamant. He said to me, "I am going to meet with those leaders, and it will all be taken care of."

So one Wednesday evening I walked with him to the meeting and waited outside the room as he addressed the doubting leaders. After embellishing my qualifications to the point of the ridiculous, he said, "Now, if you don't want Robert to be your leader, that's fine with me. I will make him my right-hand associate in the church. It's your choice."

They started talking and said, "If the pastor thinks that much of him, we should have him as our leader."

So they agreed. Dr. Criswell walked into the holding room where I was waiting, smiled, and said, "Son, it's all yours."

For the next seven years, I worked as hard as I could for him. My admiration and gratitude for this powerful figure were matched only by my fear of him! The day finally came for me to leave his staff and begin my own service as a pastor. Immediately, my status changed from servant to friend. But that change did not alter my desire for his guidance and approval. Over the next fifteen years, I would seek his advice on a variety of issues because of my deep respect for him. I mailed him birthday and anniversary cards out of love and gratitude for all he had done for me. When I learned that he was facing death, I visited with my mentor one last time. As I was selecting a tie to wear for my visit, I instinctively chose a red one, knowing it was his favorite color.

Why did I desire Dr. Criswell's approval? He could no longer fire me. The day had long since passed that he could do anything to advance my ministerial career. I wanted to please him because of my respect, reverence, and love for the man who had done so much for me.

Grace provides us with a new and superior incentive for obedience. We no longer have to fear the possibility of eternal separation from God. That issue has been settled. No condemnation awaits those of us who belong to Christ. So why should we care about pleasing Him? An even more powerful motivation for obedience than the threat of hell is the debt of gratitude we owe our Savior for all He has done for us.

"No longer do I call you slaves...but I have called you friends."

The duty to obey and the desire to obey intersect at the cross of Jesus Christ.

PART TWO

GOOD GRACE
LIVING

CHAPTER FOUR

Good Grace Spirituality

Once upon a time there was a king who fell in love with a humble maiden. The king was unsurpassed in power. Other rulers trembled at the mere mention of his name. No one dared to speak against him, for he had the ability to crush all of his opponents with a single command. Yet, for some inexplicable reason, this towering monarch chose to love a peasant girl.

But how could he ever communicate his love to her? Ironically, his greatest asset was also his greatest liability. His power could be a formidable obstacle in winning her affection. If he ordered her to be brought to the palace, crowned her as his queen, and adorned her in robes and jewels, she would submit to his request. But would she do so out of fear or love? Would she feign joy over her new life while secretly longing for the life she once had? How would the king ever know if the maiden truly loved him?

He could choose to travel to her cottage in the village. But his royal entourage might overwhelm her and frighten her away. The king already had plenty of cringing subjects who served him out of fear. What he wanted was a partner who loved him for who he was, not for his position.

Then the king had an idea. If he could not elevate the maiden without overpowering her, and if he could not travel to her home with all the pomp and circumstance that attended royal visits without scaring her, then he would meet her on her own level. The king assumed the appearance of a beggar dressed in a frayed cloak and approached her cottage. In Sören Kierkegaard's version of this tale, the king was not simply wearing a disguise. Instead, he actually changed identities. He gave up his throne in order to win the maiden's hand.[1]

The apostle Paul related another version of this tale, only Paul's version is even more dramatic—and it happens to be true. His story involves the supreme Ruler who created and now reigns over the entire universe:

Although He existed in the form of God, [Christ] did not regard
equality with God a thing to be grasped, but emptied Himself,
taking the form of a bond-servant, and being made in the likeness
of men. Being found in appearance as a man, He humbled Himself
by becoming obedient to the point of death, even death on a cross.
(Philippians 2:6-8)

The King of the universe so intensely desired to establish a relationship with you, that in some inexplicable way, He temporarily renounced His privileges as King, wrapped Himself in human flesh, endured the unfair accusations and hatred of those He had created, and actually subjected Himself to the curse each of us deserves. And why did He do this? Why was He so intent on trying to win our affection?

Because He was obligated? Monarchs have no obligations.

Because He was lonely? He already had plenty of subjects in His heavenly kingdom—think angels.

Because we *deserved* His affection? In reality, we were not "humble maidens" as in Kierkegaard's story, but rebellious servants who were constantly devising ways to defy the King's edicts.

No, the Bible gives only one reason for the King's unprecedented action: "Because of His great love with which He loved us" (Ephesians 2:4).

Neither His obligation, nor His loneliness, nor our worthiness compelled Him to make this ultimate sacrifice. Instead, for some unfathomable reason, God chose to love you with an everlasting love that cannot be quenched by your blatant disobedience toward Him or even by your callous disinterest in Him. The Bible has a word for God's underserved and unrelenting affection: grace.

Yet, amazingly, grace is often used as a weapon *against* the One who has chosen to set His affection on us. To illustrate what I mean, let's imagine a different conclusion to Kierkegaard's parable. Instead of the usual "and they lived happily ever after" ending, suppose that once the king has gained the maiden's love, he reveals his true identity to her. She responds, "I had no idea you were the king! If that's the case, I want a prenup before our marriage, guaranteeing that I get half of your fortune should I ever be unfaithful to you."

The king is shaken but agrees to the arrangement. Once the ink is dry on the document securing her share of her husband's wealth, the peasant girl exchanges her rags for Neiman Marcus suits, tears down her hut, builds a new palace, and takes a lover to occupy her time while the king is away tending to royal business.

You are unlikely to find such an ending in fairy tales because, well, they *are* fairy tales. But in reality, the alternative ending I have suggested more closely describes how many of us respond to the love of our King. Instead of viewing God's grace as a means to draw closer to Him, we use His underserved kindness as a way to take advantage of Him after we have been assured of our eternal inheritance. That is the essence of bad grace.

But good grace recognizes that the change of our status from slaves to sons and daughters and from enemies to friends should radically transform our relationship with the King. Simply put, good grace draws us toward God; bad grace alienates us from God.

Perhaps the best way to demonstrate what I mean by that statement is by contrasting how good grace and bad grace address four core components in our relationship to God.

Sin

As we saw in the second chapter, one of the residual benefits of God's grace is an awareness of sin—" 'Twas grace that taught my heart to fear." Without this consciousness of our spiritual sickness, we never would have been motivated to seek spiritual healing through Christ. But our sensitivity to sin does not disappear at our conversion; it only grows more acute as we draw closer to God.

One of the primary differences between good grace and bad grace is the perspective each position has toward sin. To be fair, both sides openly express disdain for disobedience to God. But beneath the surface, you will find a fundamental difference in the attitude toward sin.

Those who use grace as an excuse for continued disobedience have been duped by what the writer of Hebrews called "the deceitfulness of sin" (3:13). They have been deluded by the Enemy into believing that the boundaries God has placed around our behavior are meant to restrict our happiness rather than enhance it. *Oh, what fun we could have if we didn't serve such a cosmic kill-joy!* we are tempted to think. Again, go back to the question I posed in chapter 2: If you found out that God didn't exist, what would you start doing that you aren't doing now? Honestly!

Our various responses to that question not only reveal the lingering presence of a defeated—but still active—sin nature within us but also a distorted view of reality that has been the foundation of sin since the beginning of time.

In another book I described more fully how Satan deceived Eve into rebelling against her Creator. The strategy Satan employed was so wildly successful in duping the first couple that he continues to use it against us today—and it still works!

First, Satan distorted the truth about the nature of God. In effect, Satan said, "Eve, the reason God told you not to eat the forbidden fruit is that He is afraid you will become like Him, and He can't handle the competition. You had better start looking out for yourself, because He is certainly looking out for *Himself*" (see Genesis 3:4-5). The implication is obvious: God cannot be trusted because His laws are more for His benefit than for ours. God's commands concerning sex, marriage, honesty, and money are His attempts to keep us from experiencing true joy.

Martin Luther was right when he observed, "All sin is contempt of God." Every time we give in to temptation, we are registering a "no confidence" vote in the goodness and love of our Creator.

But Satan also perverted the truth about the nature of sin. Simply put, Satan attempts to make sin look better than it really is. Contradicting God's clear warning, Satan promised the woman, "If you eat of the tree, you will not die. Instead, you shall become more alive than ever. You will be like God!" Who could resist an offer like that?

Satan continues the same deception today. He no longer needs a serpent to serve as His mouthpiece to hype the beauty of sin. The media is more than willing to do his bidding. For example, whether it is through the flickering images of the latest sitcom on television or the covers of those beautiful magazines in the supermarket checkout line, we are persuaded that sex within marriage leads to boredom, but sex outside of marriage leads to exhilaration.

Simone Weil aptly described the delusion when she wrote, "Imaginary evil is romantic and varied; real evil is gloomy, monotonous, barren, boring. Imaginary good is boring; real good is always new, marvelous, intoxicating."[2]

I thought a lot about Weil's observation this week as I counseled a man who discovered the true nature of sin the hard way. Persuaded that sex with the same woman for the rest of his life was too "boring," he ventured into the world of Internet pornography. I'm sure at this point you could write the rest of the story. Soon the surreal images that were nothing more than an electronic configuration of pixels were not enough to satisfy his urges, so he began frequenting upscale "gentlemen's clubs" while on out-of-town business trips. For a while he would only watch the entertainers on stage. But after a while, just watching failed to give him the buzz he was longing for. He started visiting the VIP rooms the clubs offered for more intimate contact with the dancers. But again, such mechanical acts were not sufficient to quench his raging sexual desire. If only he could find a woman who would provide both the sexual and emotional fulfillment he longed for.

He found her, oddly enough, at church. When his wife found out about her through some sloppily hidden e-mails on the home computer, she immediately ordered her husband out of the house.

Ironically, his new lover soon decided that he really was not what she was looking for. He is now living alone in a small condominium, separated from his children and facing the dissolution of his ten-year marriage to a woman who suddenly has become all he really wants. The only problem is that she doesn't want him any longer. This man has discovered what Solomon learned from his own experience with the deceitfulness of sin:

> The lips of an adulteress drip honey
>> And smoother than oil is her speech;
> But in the end she is bitter as wormwood,
>> Sharp as a two-edged sword. (Proverbs 5:3-4)

Unlike many of our Founding Fathers, Benjamin Franklin was not a Christian. He was labeled a deist, but John Adams thought he was actually a closet atheist. But even Franklin understood a truth about sin that often escapes those with a defective view of grace. "Vicious actions are not hurtful because they are forbidden, but forbidden because they are hurtful."

REPENTANCE

Of course, even those with a proper understanding of grace are still occasionally deceived by sin. How does our occasional disobedience affect our relationship with God? What, if anything, should we do about our sin?

In a best-selling book, one representative of the bad-grace camp offers counsel that could be summarized this way: Christians don't need to ask for God's forgiveness for their sins. After all, when you trusted in Christ as your Savior, He forgave you all your sins, not just some of them. To ask God to forgive you again for sins He has already paid for insults Him.

There is a kernel of truth in what this writer says. The apostle Paul proclaimed that Christ's death was indeed sufficient to cover all, not just some, of our transgressions:

> When you were dead in your transgressions and the uncircumcision
> of your flesh, He made you alive together with Him, having for-
> given us *all* our transgressions. (Colossians 2:13)

Will you reread that verse…slowly? Substitute the word *I* for *you, me* for *you* and *us,* and *my* for *your* and *our.*

> When *I* was dead in *my* transgressions and in the uncircumcision of
> *my* flesh, he made *me* alive together with Him, having forgiven *me*
> all *my* transgressions.

Read this verse one more time, emphasizing the word *all.* That little word covers both the depth and the breadth of our disobedience. Jesus died not only for your little sins but for your big ones as well. Every act of dis-obedience, from a bad attitude at work to the act of murder, has been washed away by the blood of Jesus Christ.

Furthermore, His forgiveness covers the entire span of your life here on earth. When you trusted in Christ as your Savior, the Lord did not say to you, "All right. Everything you've done wrong up until now is forgiven. But from this point on, you'd better not mess up!" No, when Christ died for your sins two thousand years ago, *all* of your sins were still future. And that means they were *all* paid for.

You may ask, "Then why is it necessary for me to ask for God's for-giveness when I sin if I've already been forgiven?"

Advocates of bad grace fail to understand the difference between *judi-cial* and *parental* forgiveness. *Judicial forgiveness* is the one-time act of God by which He declares me "not guilty" because of the death of His Son on my behalf. The biblical term for that kind of forgiveness is *justification*.

> Therefore, having been justified by faith, we have peace with God
> through our Lord Jesus Christ. (Romans 5:1)

In an instant God's grace transformed us from being enemies of God to being children of God. Nothing we do can ever change that status because, as Paul wrote, "the gifts and the calling of God are irrevocable" (Romans 11:29). Our position in God's family is secure.

But *parental forgiveness* is altogether different. For example, imagine that your teenage son (or daughter) asks to borrow your car for a special Friday-night date. At 11:00 p.m. you receive a call telling you that your child has been arrested for drunk driving. When you arrive at the police station you not only find an inebriated teen but a car that has been totaled in a collision. You pay the bail and take your son home. Once he is sober the next morning, you read him the riot act about his behavior and announce the appropriate punishment.

Instead of admitting you are right, your son protests the punishment as too severe and tells you that he has been living under a dictatorship for sixteen years and isn't going to take it any longer. He retreats to his room, slams the door, and turns his CD player up to deafening decibels.

At this moment, how do you feel about your child? Although you don't disinherit him and throw him out on the street for his offense, a distance now exists in your day-to-day relationship with him. And that distance will continue until he is willing to admit he was wrong and asks for your forgiveness. Even if he comes to the dinner table in a good mood after spending a few hours in his room and attempts to make conversation with you, the breach in your relationship won't be healed until the issue of last night's behavior is addressed and trust is restored.

Similarly, while our sin does not alter our position in God's family, it does affect our day-to-day relationship with our heavenly Father. Until we are willing to acknowledge our disobedience and ask for God's parental forgiveness, there will be an uncomfortable distance in our relationship with God. The apostle John, who wrote to Christians, not to non-Christians, explained why:

> If we say that we have no sin, we are deceiving ourselves and the
> truth is not in us. If we confess our sins, He is faithful and righteous
> to forgive us our sins and to cleanse us from all unrighteousness. If
> we say that we have not sinned, we make Him a liar and His word
> is not in us. (1 John 1:8-10)

The biblical term for asking for God's parental forgiveness is *repentance.* The Greek word *metanoeō* denotes a change of mind that leads to a change of action. For example, this morning on the way to work, I dropped off some shirts at the dry cleaners. As I was leaving, a lady stopped me and said, "I listen to you on television every Sunday. You are absolutely brilliant!" I humbly demurred and got into my car wondering who that perceptive woman was.

I wasn't more than a block away from the dry cleaner when I looked in my rearview mirror and noticed the hood of my trunk flapping up and down. In my excitement over my new "fan," I had forgotten to retrieve my laundry basket and close the trunk. Cars whizzed past me, honking to make sure I knew I had a problem. In an instant I decided I could not continue to drive this way, so I made a U-turn, returned to the dry cleaner, and sheepishly retrieved the basket to the amusement of those in the store who had watched the whole event. I realized I had made a mistake, determined I did not want to continue in that direction, and turned around.

Bad grace limits the need for repentance to non-Christians, as if repentance were a one-time act by which unbelievers change their minds about Jesus Christ and turn to Him for salvation. But repentance is not just a one-time act that ensures heaven after we die. For a Christian, continual repentance is necessary to maintain our family relationship with God. Without it, we experience a breach in our relationship with our Father.

The first of the Ninety-five Theses that Martin Luther nailed to the church door at Wittenberg read, "When our Lord and Master Jesus Christ said 'repent,' He willed that the entire life of believers be one of repentance." For a Christian, repentance has two components.

A Change of Attitude

First, we must change our minds about our disobedience.

My friend Charles Lowery tells a story about swimming in the ocean while he was a teenager. After about twenty minutes he looked at the shoreline and noticed that his parents were no longer where they had been. Instead, they had moved their umbrellas and tent about a half mile up the beach. He then noticed that their hotel had also moved about the same distance up the beach! Obviously, neither his parents nor the hotel had moved; *he* had. Before Charles could return to his parents, he had to first acknowledge that he had drifted away from them.

The prophet Isaiah observed that "all of us like sheep have gone astray" (Isaiah 53:6). Without realizing it, all of us tend to slowly drift away from our heavenly Father until one day, like the prodigal son, we wake up and find ourselves in a distant country.

The Old Testament priest Ezra sensed that after spending seventy years of exile in a foreign land, the Israelites had drifted in their relationship with God. In Nehemiah 9, Ezra led the other priests in offering the longest recorded prayer in the Bible, which they offered on behalf of themselves and all the Israelites to restore their broken relationship with God. After recounting God's innumerable acts of grace toward the Israelites, Ezra and the priests confessed their departure from God:

> You are just in all that has come upon us;
> For You have dealt faithfully, but we have acted wickedly. (verse 33)

What does it mean to "confess our sins," a phrase the apostle John used to describe our change in attitude about our disobedience? Of all the technical theological definitions I could offer, I think the late Alan Redpath captured the true meaning when he said that confession means to quit arguing with God about your sin:

> It is a tremendous moment in a Christian's life when he can
> honestly look up into the face of God and say, "Yes, Lord, You

are right and I am wrong."… That is the thing for which God has been working in your life and in mine from the moment of our conversion.[3]

Imagine that Jesus Christ sat down with you over a cup of coffee and said, "You know how much I love you. I am so proud of you. But there is something in your life I need to talk with you about that is hurting our relationship." Do you have a pretty good idea what that "something" is that the Lord would want to discuss with you? Perhaps it's that something you are thinking about right now.

Repentance means to change your mind about the "something" that is hindering your relationship with God. Instead of arguing, rationalizing, and covering over your sin, you simply agree with God: "You're right, Lord, and I'm wrong." That change of mind, however, is incomplete without the second component of repentance…

A Change of Direction

After confessing his own sin as well as the sins of the Israelites, Ezra did not close his prayer with "Help us do better. In Jesus's name, amen." Instead, the prophet specifically detailed the ways in which he and the people had "acted wickedly," and then he led them in signing a written contract with God that included specific changes they would make in their behavior (see Nehemiah 10:28-39). Included in this contract was the promise to stop marrying unbelievers, start observing the Sabbath, and continue giving all the prescribed offerings to the Lord. The Israelites were serious about this repentance business…for a very short while!

Should we enter into written agreements with God? Some people recoil at such a suggestion. "That's legalism," they argue. "We aren't supposed to live under bondage to a contract; we are to live under grace."

However, many Christians fail to understand that we entered into a contract with God when we trusted in Christ as our Savior. This contract is called the *new covenant*. The word *covenant* means "agreement" or "contract." According to the terms of this agreement, God promises to forgive our sins on the basis of Christ's death for us. But we have responsibilities in this covenant as well, as Paul reminded the Corinthians:

> Do you not know that your body is a temple of the Holy Spirit
> who is in you, whom you have from God, and that you are not
> your own? For you have been bought with a price: therefore glorify
> God in your body. (1 Corinthians 6:19-20)

Under the terms of the new covenant, God purchased our freedom from our old slave master, Satan. The price was steep. It cost God the death of His own Son. But with our freedom comes the responsibility to obey our new Master. This commitment to obedience represents not our payment for our freedom but our gratitude for it. That's part of the deal. So the real question is not "Should I make the same kind of covenant with God that the Israelites made?" but "Am I going to fulfill the terms of the covenant I've already made with God?"

During a message I preached on Ezra's prayer—I titled the message "A Prayer for Drifters"—I gave the congregation a homework assignment. "Think about the three areas of life in which Ezra asked God for forgiveness: family life (unholy marriages), work life (failing to keep the Sabbath), and giving to God's work (ignoring the command to tithe). Ask God to reveal any ways you have failed him in these areas. Then consider writing a letter to God in which you express your genuine sorrow over your disobedience and commit to making some specific changes in your life."

The following week I received a letter from a couple in our church thanking me for the suggestion. They enclosed the following "contract" they had made with God:

Dear God, Master of the Universe, Creator of All Things:

You are truly King of Kings and Lord of Lords, and to You we give all praise....

We write to You today asking for forgiveness of our sins. Forgive us for not doing our part in Your house, which we should have done. We ask for wisdom that we may know Your will for our lives.

Our oath to God, given in faith:

1. To give our tithe, no matter what.
2. For the next three years, to give an additional 10 percent to the building fund.
3. To read our Bibles and pray each day.
4. To have a time set aside each week to pray and read together as a couple.
5. To do some kind of charity work at least once a month.
6. To practice Matthew 5:16.
7. To pray for our pastor and our church every day.

—Brian and Sherla Williams[4]

For this couple, repentance was not a legalistic obligation but a needed opportunity to return to a Father who loves them.

OBEDIENCE

If you were to ask members of the Church of Christ denomination to recite their favorite verse in the Bible, they might quote Acts 2:38: "Repent, and each of you be baptized in the name of Jesus Christ for the forgiveness of your sins." That verse represents their cornerstone belief in the necessity of baptism for salvation.

Ask Presbyterians to cite a favorite passage, and they would probably select one that deals with God's elective purpose in salvation: "He predestined us to adoption as sons through Jesus Christ to Himself, according to the kind intention of His will" (Ephesians 1:5)

Southern Baptist pastors like myself have our own favorite. "Bring the whole tithe into the storehouse" (Malachi 3:10). But if you were to ask the *members* of our congregations for their favorite verse, they would probably say Ephesians 2:8-9:

> For by grace you have been saved through faith; and that not of yourselves, it is the gift of God; not as a result of works [this is where we raise our voice for emphasis], so that no one may boast.

For several centuries we Baptists have enjoyed beating Methodists (and others) over the head with this verse as proof positive that there is no relationship between good works and salvation. We scoff at those poor souls who attempt to work themselves to the pearly gates. "Why would you ever choose a faith that is so difficult? Why not try our brand of works-free Christianity? It is so much easier." As the world's largest Protestant denomination, we (and, yes, I include myself) have also become the world's largest proponent of bad grace.

Of course we did not mean to distort grace. However, in a well-intentioned effort to avoid the error of legalism, we offer people a flavor of faith that is foreign to the New Testament: works-free Christianity. In our zeal to clarify that good works are not a prerequisite for salvation, we have unwittingly given the impression that good works in a Christian's life are like whipped cream on your Starbucks Frappuccino: nice option if you choose it, but certainly not necessary.

But the Bible never divorces faith in God's grace from obedience to His commands. Consider a few of the passages in the Bible that link faith with obedience:

He who believes in the Son has eternal life; but *he who does not obey the Son will not see life,* but the wrath of God abides on him. (John 3:36)

The word of God kept on spreading; and the number of the disciples continued to increase greatly in Jerusalem, and a great many of the priests were *becoming obedient to the faith.* (Acts 6:7)

Through [Jesus] we have received grace and apostleship to bring about *the obedience of faith* among all the Gentiles for His name's sake. (Romans 1:5)

Having been made perfect, He became *to all those who obey Him* the source of eternal salvation. (Hebrews 5:9)

New Testament scholar W. E. Vine believed that the etymological similarities between the Greek words for "obey" *(peithō)* and "trust" *(pisteuō)* are not accidental. The two concepts are closely related:

> The difference in meaning is that the former implies the obedience that is produced by the latter, cf. Heb. 3:18, 19, where the disobedience of the Israelites is said to be the evidence of their unbelief.… When a man obeys God he gives the only possible evidence that in his heart he believes God.… *Peithō* ["obey"] in N.T. suggests an actual and outward result of the inward persuasion and consequent faith.[5]

Obedience is the visible result of faith. The apostle Paul said virtually the same thing in Ephesians 2. The problem is that we Baptists always stop short when quoting this passage. To really understand what Paul was saying about the relationship between grace and works, let's read one verse further:

> For by grace you have been saved through faith; and that not of yourselves, it is the gift of God; not as a result of works so that no one may boast. For we are His workmanship, created in Christ Jesus *for good works,* which God prepared beforehand so *that we would walk in them.* (Ephesians 2:8-10)

What a difference a little preposition like "by" can make! Paul, the champion of grace, affirmed that we are not saved by good works, but *by* grace. Those who attempt to gain entrance into heaven *by* their good works are in for a rude awakening one day.

But Paul didn't stop there. He explained that we were saved *for* good works. We are God's workmanship *(poeima* in Greek from which we derive the word *poem).* Your life is a poem, a masterpiece that God is creating. Your salvation is not the end of His plan for your life, but the beginning! Your conversion is just the first line of the unique story God is writing about you. Chuck Swindoll expressed that truth this way:

> From His sovereign seat, God foresaw us resting in His protection and boldly taking a stand against evil, compassionately extending a hand to the needy, and lovingly sharing the gospel every time He gives us a chance. His plan for our lives extends beyond salvation to sanctification, beyond standing in grace to walking in good deeds.[6]

What is the relationship between faith and works?

Suppose I invite you to my backyard one beautiful spring afternoon to show you my apple tree. "Have you ever seen a tree so full of life?" I gush.

"Full of life? It's dead!" you observe as you look at the barren branches.

"Dead?" I protest. "How could you say such a judgmental thing about my tree?"

"It's obviously dead because it has no apples on its branches," you explain.

Embarrassed over your observation, I say, "Wait just a moment, and I'll fix that."

I run into my kitchen and return with some apples I purchased from the local supermarket, and I tie them to the branches.

"Now it's alive!" I proclaim.

I doubt my actions would change your conclusion about the condition of my tree. Trees that are alive produce fruit. It's not that the fruit *makes* the tree alive, but the fruit *proves* that the tree is alive. Furthermore, tying apples to a dead apple-tree branch does nothing to imbue that branch with life.

What is true in the world of horticulture is also true in the spiritual realm. Jesus said that people who are spiritually alive will naturally produce fruit.

> Bear fruit in keeping with repentance.… [For] every tree that does
> not bear good fruit is cut down and thrown into the fire. (Matthew
> 3:8,10)

In a well-intentioned but misguided effort to uphold the doctrine of salvation by grace alone, I have tried to make excuses for people who profess to be Christians but have no interest in the Bible, find it difficult and even painful to endure a worship service, have never shared their faith with anyone, and live in continued disobedience to God.

"Yes, they are saved, but they just haven't matured in their faith," I would rationalize.

"No!" Jesus exclaims. There is only one word for spiritually unfruitful people: dead.

Furthermore, "tying on" some good works does not make a spiritually dead person alive any more than tying apples to a barren branch imparts life to that branch.

Good grace affirms that while obedience to God's commands does not *secure* our salvation, it does *verify* our salvation. James, the half brother of Jesus, said it this way: "Faith, if it has no works, is dead" (James 2:17). John Calvin, who fought any attempts to add works as a requisite for salvation, nevertheless understood the role of good works in authenticating our faith: "It is therefore faith alone which justifies, and yet the faith which justifies is not alone."[7]

Good grace understands that obedience to God's commands is not just nice; it's absolutely necessary for a true follower of Christ.

REWARDS

True or false? God treats all His children the same.

Your answer depends upon your view of grace. Bad grace insists that God never favors one of His children over another. Grace, after all, means that there is nothing you can do to make God love you any more or any less than He already does. To believe otherwise puts undue pressure on Christians to earn God's love. Such a performance-based faith causes undue stress and alienates us from God. "God is much more interested in who you are than in what you do," these folks insist.

Although such statements are common among many Christians, are they accurate? Does God treat all His children the same? Do *you* treat each of your children the same?

- Aren't you more likely to give an obedient child more privileges and perks than a disobedient child?

- Wouldn't you be more likely to grant the requests of a grateful child than an ungrateful one?
- Isn't your heart warmer toward the child who expresses affection for you than it is toward the child who is indifferent toward you?

Why would we assume that our heavenly Father is any different? After all, we were created in His image. Just because we are not like God in *every* way does not mean we are not like God in *any* way.

One characteristic of bad grace is the belief that our actions have no consequences in this life or the next. The Christian who is faithful to his mate is no more welcomed into God's presence than the Christian who lives in adultery. The believer who invests her resources in God's kingdom has no more advantages than the Christian who keeps his money for himself. Someone who regularly shares her faith with others will experience the same heaven as the one who never shares his faith with anyone. God's kingdom is the ultimate democracy where all citizens are treated equally—or so we are led to believe.

But such an idea is foreign to the Bible. A proper view of grace teaches us that while there is nothing we can do to earn God's forgiveness, there are many things we can do to gain God's approval and rewards.

For example, the Bible teaches that a Christian who follows God's commands is more likely to have her prayers answered than one who disregards His commands:

> For the eyes of the Lord are toward the righteous, and His ears attend to their prayer. But the face of the Lord is against those who do evil. (1 Peter 3:12)

The person who faithfully invests in God's work will enjoy more of God's favor than the person who robs God by withholding his gifts:

"You are cursed with a curse, for you are robbing Me, the whole
nation of you! Bring the whole tithe into the storehouse, so that
there may be food in My house, and test Me now in this," says the
LORD of hosts, "if I will not open for you the windows of heaven
and pour out for you a blessing until it overflows." (Malachi 3:9-10)

The believer who observes Communion in a reverential way will live a
healthier—and longer—life than the one who approaches the Lord's Table
in an irreverent way:

A man must examine himself, and in so doing he is to eat of the
bread and drink of the cup. For he who eats and drinks, eats and
drinks judgment to himself if he does not judge the body rightly.
For this reason many among you are weak and sick, and a number
sleep. (1 Corinthians 11:28-30)

Our actions *do* have consequences not only in this world but also in
the next one. Contrary to popular opinion, heaven will not be the same for
all Christians. Obedient Christians will receive greater rewards than those
Christians who neglect God's commands.

No man can lay a foundation other than the one which is laid,
which is Jesus Christ. Now if any man builds on the foundation with
gold, silver, precious stones, wood, hay, straw, each man's work will
become evident; for the day will show it because it is to be revealed
with fire, and the fire itself will test the quality of each man's work.
If any man's work which he has built on it remains, he will receive a
reward. If any man's work is burned up, he will suffer loss; but he
himself will be saved, yet so as through fire. (1 Corinthians 3:11-15)

In my book *As Time Runs Out,* I illustrated Paul's words with this analogy:

> Imagine that your father, a multibillionaire, purchases two one-acre tracts of land for you and a sibling. He pours a foundation on each piece of land and then gives each of you one million dollars, with these instructions: "I am going to give you one year to build the most beautiful house you can construct. At the end of the year, the one who builds the most elaborate house will receive twice as much of my estate as the other." You and your sibling are thrilled with the possibility.
>
> You begin work immediately. You hire architects to draw up the plans, you ask contractors for estimates, and you establish a rigid schedule to make sure you complete your work on time. When the deadline arrives, you have a home that rivals the Taj Mahal.
>
> Your sibling, however, is not as industrious. Family responsibilities, work, and hobbies keep him from the task at hand. Not only that, but he has some immediate needs for that million dollars: college tuition, a new car, and a swimming pool to mention just a few. The night before the deadline, he decides to get busy and construct the best home he can with little money and only a few hours of time. A grass hut is all he can manage to build.
>
> The next morning your father surveys the two homes. He praises you for your efforts and rewards you with the promise of a large portion of his vast estate. As he walks around your sibling's grass hut, however, he expresses his disappointment. As a result of procrastination and squandering of resources, your sibling forfeited billions of dollars of future wealth. He is still in the family, but he does not receive the same reward.[8]

Paul was saying that as Christians we all have the same foundation for our lives: Jesus Christ. Nevertheless, we choose the kind of life we build upon that foundation. Some choose to build palaces and receive a greater share of their Father's wealth; others squander their time and resources and build grass huts, forfeiting future rewards.

Occasionally I hear someone say, "I don't care anything about rewards in heaven. I'll be happy just to make it in." But according to Paul, those who surrender their rewards will suffer real, measurable loss (see 1 Corinthians 3:15), just as the negligent brother did. These rewards, which include special privileges in heaven (see 2 Peter 1:11 and Revelation 2:7), praise from our Father (see Matthew 25:21), and positions of responsibility (see 2 Timothy 2:12 and Matthew 25:21) are worth working and sacrificing for.

But are blessings in this life and rewards in the next really a proper motivation for obeying God? The apostle Paul thought so! In 2 Corinthians 5:9, Paul wrote what should be the purpose statement of every believer: "We...have as our ambition, whether at home or absent, to be pleasing to [God]."

Then in the next verse, Paul stated his motivation for wanting to please God. Gratitude for his salvation? Obligation as one of God's creatures? Desire to glorify God in the world? No, it was the promise of future rewards:

We must all appear before the judgment seat of Christ, so that
each one may be recompensed [rewarded] for his deeds in the
body, ac-cording to what he has done, whether good or bad.
(2 Corinthians 5:10)

Paul firmly believed that heaven would not be the same for everyone. Those who endured "momentary, light affliction" for Christ—which, for Paul, included beatings, imprisonment, and ultimately, death—would be more than compensated by the Master with the "eternal weight of glory far beyond all comparison" (2 Corinthians 4:17). One writer said that when compared to the glory of heaven, the worst horrors of this earth will be viewed as no more than a one-night stay in an inconvenient hotel.

That promise of future rewards captivated Paul's imagination and motivated his obedience until the end of his earthly existence. As he faced his execution, he penned this epitaph for himself, which is now engraved in stone in a little chapel outside Rome, marking the place where the apostle was beheaded:

> I have fought the good fight, I have finished the course, I have kept the faith; in the future there is laid up for me the crown of righteousness, which the Lord, the righteous Judge, will award to me on that day; and not only to me, but also to all who have loved His appearing. (2 Timothy 4:7-8)

Now you may say, "But Robert, isn't serving God for rewards a selfish motivation? Shouldn't we obey Him because of our desire to glorify His name?"

I love how Matthew Henry answered that question: "God has been pleased therein to twist interests with us, so that in seeking his glory we really and effectually seek our own true interests."

To take God at His Word, believing that He will ultimately—but not always immediately—honor those who serve Him, is the essence of faith. And as the writer of the book of Hebrews declared,

> Without faith it is impossible to please Him, for he who comes to God must believe that He is and that He is a rewarder of those who seek Him. (11:6)

Good grace understands that obedience matters. Actions do have consequences, both in this life and in the one to come.

CHAPTER FIVE

Good Grace
Decision Making

Let's begin this chapter by taking a quiz. Mark the following statements as either true or false:

1. You can be a dedicated Christian and drink alcoholic beverages on a regular basis. True or false?
2. It's best for Christians not to shop on Sundays. True or false?
3. Christian parents should discourage their children from celebrating Halloween. True or false?
4. Children should not read Harry Potter novels. True or false?
5. Homeschooling is preferable to public schooling. True or false?
6. Christian hymns are usually more worshipful than contemporary Christian music. True or false?

What are the correct answers to these questions? *Are* there correct answers? I can see some of you turning red with indignation at this point. You may protest, "Everyone knows that the Bible clearly teaches that _____ is wrong!" or "Any committed Christian knows that _____ is better than _____!" Really? If the answers to these questions are obvious, why are Christians so divided over these issues?

These questions have one thing in common: They deal with the gray areas of life. By *gray areas* I am referring to those questions for which the Bible gives no specific answers. Of course, folks who have strong opinions about certain issues will usually claim that the Bible *does* address their pet concerns. However, when pressed they usually cannot cite any passage of Scripture that relates specifically to the subject, or they are forced to extrapolate a current application from some ancient (and often unrelated) command.

For example, those who object to Christians reading Harry Potter novels will cite passages in the Bible condemning witchcraft and sorcery and conclude, "Since God hates occult practices, and Harry Potter novels are about sorcery, Christians shouldn't read them." Whether or not such a conclusion is correct, it should be clear that it comes not from a direct command of Scripture but from an application of Scripture.

Is this proper use of the Bible? Even if I conclude that Harry is wrong for me, can I also conclude that he is wrong for other people? How do I decide about questionable issues that the Bible does not specifically address?

So far we have seen that good grace frees us to serve a new Master, not *no* master. Good grace does not exempt us from obedience; it obligates and empowers us to an even greater obedience to God's commands concerning our spiritual lives, our marriages, our relationships, and our responsibilities in the church.

But how does a proper understanding of grace impact our decisions regarding the gray areas of life for which there are no specific biblical commands? Should I allow the prejudices and ignorance of others to dictate my behavior? Does grace allow me to thumb my nose at the legalists who decry drinking, dancing, and Harry Potter novels?

Those who pervert the doctrine of grace usually go to one of two extremes regarding life's gray areas. Legalists insist that there are no gray areas. Every question about conduct is clearly answered in Scripture, if you will search diligently enough and learn how to read between the lines. Of course, the "clear answers" to these questions always conveniently coincide with the legalist's personal opinions. Max Lucado highlights the primary flaw of legalism: "Legalism makes my opinion your burden, makes my opinion your boundary, makes my opinion your obligation."

But libertarians, who resist any binding standard of conduct, engage in an equally dangerous distortion of grace regarding these questionable areas of behavior. Some want to label *every* area "gray," even when the Bible specifically addresses the topic.

For example, many times I have counseled with husbands or wives who insist they are praying about whether to divorce their mate. "Has your mate deserted you or committed adultery?" I will ask. More often than not, the answer to both questions is no. Yet even though the person lacks biblical grounds for ending the marriage, he or she still wrestles with a question for which the Bible already gives an answer. Why? Like most of us, the person naturally rebels against the idea that "one principle fits all" and wants to believe that his or her situation is unique and deserves special consideration.

However, the more common response of libertarians to the gray areas is to refuse to allow anyone else's opinion to govern their conduct. Unless an issue is clearly answered in the Bible, they argue, every Christian is free to seek God's direction (which usually means doing whatever one wants to do) without regard for anyone else's convictions. Furthermore, the libertarian justifies the flouting of other people's feelings with a pseudospirituality:

- "I refuse to allow anyone to place me under the law."
- "I am following Christ, not man."
- "As a more mature Christian, I understand that I have the freedom to _____. As you grow in grace, you will discover that freedom too."

However, the apostle Paul rejected both extreme approaches to the gray areas of conduct. While he had no sympathy for legalism, which attempted to place Christians under bondage to either manufactured or outdated codes of conduct (read the book of Galatians for Paul's complete discourse on this subject), he also condemned the idea of individualism that elevates personal freedom above the feelings and needs of others.

What standard should govern our decisions regarding these doubtful areas of conduct? To answer that question we need to take a trip to the meat market.

MEAT-MARKET CHRISTIANITY

For Christians living in the city of Corinth, going to R-rated movies, observing Halloween, and having wine before dinner were not hot topics of debate. However, the believers residing in that wealthy port city had their own gray area of conduct, which had divided their church: Should Christians eat meat that had been sacrificed to an idol?

A little background information is helpful to understand the Corinthians' dilemma. Both the Greeks and Romans had gods for every part of life. There was a god of war, a god of love, a god of travel, a god of justice. In fact, there was a god for just about every facet of life. The best way to win favor with the gods was to offer them food through sacrifices (kind of like leaving cookies and milk for Santa Claus). These meat sacrifices offered to the gods were usually divided into three parts: One-third was consumed by the fire, one-third was given to the priest, and the remaining third could be eaten by the person offering the sacrifice.

Obviously, the priests could not eat all the meat left for them, so they would sell it at a market located within the temple. This meat was highly valued because, having been part of a sacrifice, it was thought to be cleansed of demons. (Picture the label: *No Fat, No Demons.*)

The question facing the Corinthian Christians was "Should we eat this meat which has been offered to an idol?" New Christians in the church had come out of an idolatrous lifestyle and strongly objected to eating anything that had been offered to a counterfeit god. To them, this meat represented an old way of life from which they had been delivered. To start eating this meat again, as they had done when they were unbelievers, would be tantamount to returning to idolatry.

However, some of the more mature believers in the church understood that idols were powerless. So if they could purchase the meat at a good price or if someone served it to them for dinner, what harm—other than some unnecessary cholesterol—could there be in enjoying it?

Obviously, this is not a raging controversy among Christians today. You probably won't find an aisle in your local supermarket labeled "Meat Offered to Idols." But there are equally questionable issues in our day that confuse and divide Christians:

- Is it permissible to worship on Saturday evenings rather than on Sunday mornings?
- Should Christians practice birth control?
- Should those who have divorced and remarried—even for biblical reasons—be allowed to serve in leadership positions in the church?
- Is it permissible for a Christian to consume alcoholic beverages in moderation?
- Should Christians participate in Easter egg hunts?

Some Christians would shout "No!" to each of these questions, while others would cite grace as a reason for responding yes. But based on Paul's words to the Corinthians regarding the meat issue, he would probably respond, "It depends."

Depends on what? So glad you asked!

Good Grace and the Gray Areas of Life

Instead of answering the Corinthians' questions about meat offered to idols with a yes or no, Paul outlined three principles to consider when deciding about the gray areas of life. Advocates of bad grace will always say that they are free to do anything they desire as long as they are not violating a specific command of Scripture (or one of their own arbitrary rules).

However, as Paul explains in 1 Corinthians 8, good grace recognizes that decisions about questionable practices should be made from a higher perspective than personal preferences. Specifically...

Good Grace Elevates Love Above Knowledge

The "bad gracers" in the Corinthian church were using doctrinal knowledge as a basis for eating the meat in question: "Unlike 'baby Christians,' we know that idols are insignificant. Why should we allow the ignorance of these new converts to limit our freedom?"

Today you might hear similar proclamations:

- "We know that we no longer live under Sabbath restrictions."
- "We know there is nothing inherently sinful about alcohol."
- "We know we have the freedom to watch this movie or read that book."

Paul never questioned the doctrinal correctness of these more "mature" believers. In fact, he agreed with their assessment about the meat offered to idols:

Concerning the eating of things sacrificed to idols, we know that there is no such thing as an idol in the world, and that there is no God but one. (1 Corinthians 8:4)

But as important as doctrinal knowledge is, there is something just as vital: love for God and for other people. In fact, without that love, our knowledge is worthless:

Knowledge makes arrogant, but love edifies. If anyone supposes that
he knows anything, he has not yet known as he ought to know; but
if anyone loves God, he is known by Him. (1 Corinthians 8:1-3)

Biblical knowledge is essential, but it is not enough. Any information
we possess about the Bible that does not lead us to love God or others more
deeply is useless. No, on second thought, it is *lethal*. Why? Knowledge
without love leads to arrogance.

Do you know Christians who are intoxicated with biblical knowledge
or enamored with some system of theology and yet lack any genuine concern for other people? It is possible to become "puffed up" (the meaning of
arrogance) with knowledge instead of love.

Confession time. I am what some would call a *fundamentalist* in my
theology. I have hung around with other fundamentalists throughout my
ministry. While I appreciate the genuine devotion that those in our group
have to the authority and sufficiency of the Bible, we have mistakenly
equated doctrinal fidelity with genuine spirituality. I think some Christians
really believe that when we stand before the judgment seat of Christ, the
Lord is going to hand each of us a blue exam book and ask us to draw a
chart of the end times, give ten evidences of the Virgin Birth, and explain
the difference between Calvinism and Arminianism.

In truth, God's evaluation of our lives will consist of only one question:
How well did we exhibit the attitudes, actions, and affections of Jesus Christ?

Don't misunderstand what I am saying. Correct doctrinal knowledge
is essential to resembling Christ in every aspect of our lives. We cannot
apply truth we don't know. Unfortunately, it is far too easy to know truth
we don't apply.

Paul reminded the Corinthians—and succeeding generations of Christians—that all doctrinal knowledge should lead us to love God more

intently. And a genuine love of God will lead to a genuine concern for people. You can't have one without the other:

> If someone says, "I love God," and hates his brother, he is a liar; for the one who does not love his brother whom he has seen, cannot love God whom he has not seen. (1 John 4:20)

What does this have to do with eating demonproof meat—or drinking one hundred proof alcohol? When answering the question "Should I or shouldn't I?" Paul says we must ask not only "What does the Bible say?" but also "How will my actions impact other people?" Those who ask only the first question without considering the well-being of others do not have as much spiritual understanding as they claim.

And that leads to a second principle to consider when deciding about the gray areas of life.

Good Grace Elevates the Welfare of Others Above My Personal Freedom

The newer converts in Corinth did not possess the same spiritual understanding that the more mature believers had. Some of these new Christians still believed in the existence of many gods:

> Not all men have this knowledge; but some, being accustomed to the idol until now, eat food as if it were sacrificed to an idol; and their conscience being weak is defiled. (1 Corinthians 8:7)

You might wonder, "How could they be genuine Christians and still believe in idols?" Although these new Christians believed there was one true God, they did not yet understand there was only one *real* God. They still believed that idols possessed power.

Today people are constantly adding to what someone must do or believe to become a Christian. I have heard people say, "You can't be a Christian and deny the Virgin Birth, believe in evolution, be pro-choice, or reject the inerrancy of the Bible." Of course you can! You can be an untaught Christian, a misled Christian, or even a disobedient Christian. But you are still a Christian if you have placed your faith in Christ for the forgiveness of your sins. In Acts 16 Paul told the Philippian jailer there is only one thing a person must believe in to receive forgiveness: "Believe in the Lord Jesus, and you will be saved" (verse 31).

The fact that these new Christians were still untaught "babies" meant that the more mature believers in the congregation should have *more* concern for their well-being, not less. After all, don't we tend to offer more care and protection to infants than we do to teenagers or adults?

Unfortunately, by exercising their freedom to eat meat offered to idols, the "mature" believers were inflicting serious injury on the newer converts by leading them to violate their conscience:

> But some, being accustomed to the idol until now, eat food as if it
> were sacrificed to an idol; and their conscience being weak is defiled.
> (1 Corinthians 8:7)

Many people speak about conscience with little understanding of what it is. Our conscience is like an internal warning system that governs our behavior. Whenever we get close to someone or something that could lead us into sin, the *beep...beep...beep* begins to sound. John MacArthur describes our conscience this way: "Conscience is God's doorkeeper to keep us out of places where we could be harmed. As we mature, conscience allows us to go more places and to do more things because we will have more spiritual strength and better spiritual judgment."[1]

When our oldest daughter, Julia, was five, she was always wanting to walk by herself to a friend's house a few streets from our home. Out of concern for her safety, we never allowed her to walk alone. She was too young for that kind of independence. However, as I was working on this chapter, I interrupted my writing to purchase a car for Julia, who just turned sixteen. I admit that I was more than a little apprehensive about turning the keys over to her, but it was time. She had become mature enough to make good decisions.

Our conscience is a God-given guardian to warn us of situations that could lead us into sin. The conscience of new Christians is often highly sensitive, which helps keep them away from practices that could easily pull them back into their old way of life. But as their faith strengthens and matures, the people, places, or patterns of behavior that at one time might have led them into a sinful lifestyle are no longer a temptation.

When we ignore our conscience and wander beyond the behavioral boundaries that God has established for our protection, we risk being attacked and abducted by the Enemy. That is why Paul warned Timothy (and all of us) to keep "a good conscience, which some have rejected and suffered shipwreck in regard to their faith" (1 Timothy 1:19). To ignore our conscience is as foolish as ignoring a shark warning posted on a beach. Those who travel beyond the boundaries are subject to devastating assaults.

So what does all this have to do with eating meat offered to idols? As I mentioned earlier, to the new converts in the Corinthian church, this meat represented the former way of life from which they had been delivered. For them to start eating this meat again might lead them back into idolatry. Anytime they even got close to a pagan temple or to the food sacrificed in it, the *beep...beep...beep* began to sound in their consciences. They knew they should stay as far away as possible.

However, when they saw more mature Christians in the church feasting on idol meat, they were tempted to ignore their internal warning systems and indulge in a thick, juicy "idol burger" with their fellow church members. The danger of ignoring our conscience just once is that we find it's much easier to ignore it again…and again…and again…until we wake up one day and wonder how we have moved so far away from God.

Although eating this idol meat meant nothing more than a delicious dinner to the more established believers, to the new converts it represented the beginning of a downward spiral into their old way of life. Thus, by exercising their freedom, the more mature Corinthians had inflicted serious harm on these new Christians.

I need to pause here and correct a common misunderstanding that frequently emerges from this passage. Legalists in the church who want to transform opinions into a code of conduct will often use the "weaker brother" argument to govern our behavior. "Since I object to _____, you can't do it because you are causing me to stumble," the legalist will argue.

But notice in this passage that those Paul described as weak and harmed by our reckless exercise of freedom are not the ones objecting to our behavior and steadfastly refusing to engage in it themselves. Instead, weaker Christians are the ones who say, "Even though I think this is wrong, I will do it anyway, since _____ is doing it, and he is a strong believer."

Just because someone in the church may object to what you do is no reason to restrict your freedom in Christ. As one of my seminary professors used to say, the church is filled with professional "weaker brothers" who love to criticize every move we make. You can never make everyone happy, so quit trying. As Bill Cosby once observed, "I don't know the key to success, but the key to failure is trying to please everybody."

Paul was not advocating a lifestyle in which we attempt to please everyone, but he was encouraging us to consider how our behavior might impact the spiritual health of other believers, especially those who are young in their faith.

And that leads to a third principle regarding the gray areas of life.

Good Grace Elevates God's Interests Above My Desires

Bad grace exalts personal freedom over every other consideration. My right to do whatever I please overrides any concern for what others may need or what God may desire. Yet, to paraphrase John Donne, no Christian is an island unto himself. Instead, we are "Christ's body and individually members of it" (1 Corinthians 12:27). Because of our spiritual connection to other believers who form the body of Christ, our actions impact other believers in the body as well as the Head of the body, Jesus Christ. That means when our choices lead another Christian to sin, we've not only harmed that believer, but we've actually injured every other part of the body, including Jesus, our Head.

> And so, by sinning against the brethren and wounding their conscience when it is weak, you sin against Christ. (1 Corinthians 8:12)

Furthermore, since we are part of this spiritual organism called the body of Christ, when we inflict harm on another member of the body, we are actually hurting ourselves. As Paul reminded the Corinthians,

> If one member suffers, all the members suffer with it; if one member is honored, all the members rejoice with it. Now you are Christ's body, and individually members of it. (1 Corinthians 12:26-27)

Can you imagine any circumstance in which you would take a hammer and purposefully smash your right thumb or, even worse, hit yourself in the head just for the fun of it? Yet when we knowingly engage in behavior that leads a fellow member of Christ's body to defile his or her conscience and fall away from God, that's just as insane as swinging that hammer.

I realize that such a thought runs contrary to our cultural emphasis on individualism. Many churches resemble clubs in which participants who share a common interest (spirituality) show up once a week for an hour or so, hear a presentation, and slip out without any meaningful interaction with others. However, we mistakenly assume that the lack of connection between believers in the visible church mirrors a similar disconnection in the invisible (or universal) church.

Whether or not we realize it, we *are* connected to every other believer in the world and in heaven, as well as to Jesus Christ. And that means our behavior does have consequences. Either we are building up or we are destroying this invisible but very real body for which Jesus Christ gave His life.

That realization led Paul to this conclusion regarding the controversy over idol meat:

> If food causes my brother to stumble, I will never eat meat
> again, so that I will not cause my brother to stumble. (1 Corinthi-
> ans 8:13)

Paul was in essence saying, "Yes, grace provides freedom. But my personal freedom ends when it harms a fellow Christian and therefore harms Christ."

THREE QUESTIONS FOR GOOD GRACE DECISION MAKING

Paul didn't stop with a pious-sounding platitude. Instead, he offers us three filters we should use when making decisions about behavioral gray areas:

> All things are lawful, but not all things are profitable. All things are
> lawful, but not all things edify. Let no one seek his own good, but

that of his neighbor.... Whether, then, you eat or drink or whatever
you do, do all to the glory of God. (1 Corinthians 10:23-24,31)

"Is This Behavior Lawful?"

Paul assumed that the behavior in question was lawful—that there was no
precise scriptural injunction against it. Thus, the first question we need to
ask ourselves about questionable behavior should be, "What does the Bible
say about this issue?" or to put it another way, "Is this gray area really gray?"
As we have already seen, the New Testament provides many guidelines
regarding morality, relationships, and responsibilities to God's kingdom
that should direct our choices. Grace does not exempt us from those
requirements; it empowers us to meet those requirements.

However, unlike the Old Covenant, which provided answers for every
conceivable life situation, the New Testament usually provides us with general principles that we must learn to apply to our specific questions. For
example, I can search the New Testament from Matthew to the maps and
never find an answer to the question, "Should I attend a James Bond
movie?" Yet the New Testament does provide this principle:

Flee from youthful lusts and pursue righteousness, faith, love and
peace, with those who call on the Lord from a pure heart. (2 Timothy 2:22)

If I am sincerely attempting to become a more obedient disciple of
Christ, then I would ask myself, "Does this movie, television program,
novel, or activity incite or extinguish the youthful lusts that the Bible says
I am to avoid?" The libertarian will answer, "If there is no verse prohibiting it, I am free to do it." The legalist will reply, "I have the answer for you,
and here it is." But the practitioner of good grace understands that every
Christian must answer such a question for himself or herself.

"Is This Behavior Profitable?"

As the leader of a large organization, I have a great deal of freedom regarding how I spend my time. No one is looking over my shoulder and telling me what to do. I do not fill out a time sheet. I could probably spend hours hidden away in my study reading novels or playing video games, and no one would be the wiser. But I don't do these things. Why not? The leadership and members to whom I am accountable do have general expectations about my performance: that I will prepare meaningful sermons, give direction to the church, and care for members' spiritual needs. Eventually my slothfulness would be exposed.

But an even more compelling reason for not squandering my time is that it doesn't move me toward my goals in life. I have a passion for preaching and leadership that compels me to make the best use of my time.

The apostle Paul counseled that when we evaluate out behavior, we should ask the simple question, "Is this behavior profitable?" Or put another way, "How will this use of my time and energy move me toward my God-given passion in life?" Obviously, Paul was assuming that our overriding purpose in life is to glorify God by building up rather than destroying His kingdom. If the Great Commission—adding to the kingdom of God by encouraging unbelievers to become obedient disciples of Christ—is our primary passion, then a lot of activities will be weeded out by the "Is it profitable?" question.

"Is This Behavior Helpful?"

Even if the other two filter questions give me a green light to engage in a certain behavior, how will it affect my fellow Christians? My behavior may be lawful. It could even be construed as profitable if for no other reason than it allows me the relaxation and refreshment necessary to recharge my batteries as I pursue my God-given purpose in life.

But does this behavior edify or build up other Christians? This question is the crux of Paul's answer to the meat dilemma, not because it always give us the most definitive answer, but because it is usually the question we are least likely to consider.

When I was in high school, the mother of one of the girls in our church youth group stopped me after the evening service and said, "My daughter went to the movies the other night and was horrified at the terrible language in the film. She had never heard such language in her life."

I could not figure out why she was telling me about her daughter's experience unless it was because she considered me to be such a spiritual giant in our group. So I took the bait and asked, "If the movie was so bad, why did your daughter go?" Once the mom had me hooked, she replied, "Well, a week earlier she was driving past the theater and saw you and your date waiting in line to see the film. She reasoned to herself, 'If this movie is okay for Robert Jeffress, then it must be okay for me.'" I quickly looked for the nearest pew to crawl under.

None of us lives in a vacuum. The choices we make have a profound impact on others and therefore on the kingdom of God. Our decisions either encourage others to be fully devoted followers of Christ or discourage them.

That realization provides most of the guidance we need when considering the gray areas of behavior.

CHAPTER SIX

Good Grace Relationships

Business and friendship don't mix," Laura's husband had warned her. How she wished she had listened to Dave's advice before she partnered with her best friend, Janet, in a small home-based business. "Memories Forever," a concept for teaching women how to make scrapbooks, was designed for stay-at-home moms who wanted to earn some extra cash. Laura and Janet, who had been friends since grade school, loved the idea of working together in a venture that allowed them to use their artistic bent and required little start-up capital. They immediately opened a joint checking account, and each deposited five hundred dollars.

After the first month of operation, they sat down at Laura's kitchen table and analyzed their profits and losses. Their initial one-thousand-dollar investment had dwindled to four hundred dollars. However, since any business required some nonrecurring start-up costs, they weren't too discouraged. After the second month, they not only recouped their initial investment, but they had added another thousand dollars to their balance. Things were looking up!

When Laura opened up the bank statement for their third month of operation, she was surprised to see that the balance the bank showed was three hundred dollars less than her own records showed. She examined the statement more closely and noted three separate ATM withdrawals for one hundred dollars each. Knowing that she had not used her card, she quickly telephoned Janet. Perhaps Janet's ATM card had been stolen.

"No," Janet said. "There were some miscellaneous expenses for the business that required cash. I'm sorry I forgot to tell you."

Laura asked if Janet would give her the receipts since she was responsible for the bookkeeping chores.

"You don't trust me?" Janet snapped.

"Of course I trust you, but we agreed we needed to keep good records," Laura countered. Laura had not even considered that anything was wrong until Janet's unwarranted outburst. A week later, when she casually mentioned the receipts, Janet said that she had misplaced them.

The next month Janet made two more unauthorized withdrawals, offered another flimsy explanation, and again, had no receipts. Laura did not want to think the worst about her best friend, but how could she ignore the mounting evidence that Janet was embezzling their funds?

One day Laura received a phone call from an officer at their bank informing her that one of her company checks had bounced. "I don't understand how that could have happened, but I'll be right over to see what needs to be done."

An hour later Laura received the jolt for which she was not prepared. In examining the most recent batch of canceled checks for "Memories Forever," she came across one made out to First National Mortgage Company for fifteen hundred dollars and signed by Janet. No wonder the check to their supplier had been returned.

Laura didn't call Janet ahead of time but drove as quickly as she could to Janet's house. Ignoring any pleasantries, Laura confronted Janet with the check.

"I'm so sorry," Janet said as she began to sob. "Jeff had his hours cut in half three months ago, and we were too ashamed to tell people we were hurting financially. At first I used the withdrawals to help pay for food. But then there was no money for our mortgage payment, and I panicked. I always meant to pay it back. Please forgive me."

Forgive her? Of course Laura would forgive her longtime friend. But what about their business, which was now one thousand dollars in the hole? Someone had to make up the deficit, and do it quickly. Should Laura dissolve their partnership immediately? Should the two families meet and work out a repayment plan? Should they continue their venture but remove Janet's name from the bank account for stricter control? Laura dreaded talking to her husband about the problem and hearing the inevitable "I told you so," so she confided in Debbie, her small-group leader at church.

Debbie, who was very wise in spiritual matters, reminded Laura of a story Jesus told in Matthew 18. "Do you remember the parable Jesus told about a slave who owed a debt he could never repay? After the slave begged the king for mercy, the king forgave the slave's debt.

"Then the slave went out and found a fellow slave who owed him a small amount of money, but he refused to forgive his fellow slave of the paltry sum. When the king heard about it, he called the first slave in and said, 'How could you who have been forgiven so much refuse to forgive such a little debt?' In the same way, Jesus said, we who have been forgiven so much by God have an obligation to forgive others."

"Does that mean I shouldn't insist that Janet repay the money she stole?" Laura asked.

"Does God insist that you pay for your sins on the installment plan before He forgives you?" Debbie countered.

"Do you think I should continue in business with Janet after what she has done?"

"Laura, when God forgave you, did He say, 'I forgive you, but I will never trust you again'?"

"Wouldn't it be wise, then, to at least build in some controls over our finances so that this doesn't happen again?" Laura wondered.

"What kinds of strings did God place on His forgiveness of you?" Debbie asked. "Just as God forgave us unconditionally, we are to forgive others."

Who could argue with that kind of logic? Laura's husband, Dave, for one. He said that kind of argument was fine for the Sunday-school classroom, but it didn't apply in the business world. Refusing to make Janet repay her debt and continuing their business arrangement with no changes would be tantamount to hanging a Kick Me sign around Laura's neck. When Laura used Debbie's analogy of how God forgives us unconditionally, Dave snapped, "Yeah, but we're not God."

How does a proper understanding of grace impact our relationships with those who mistreat us? Does forgiveness require us to overlook their offenses completely? Should others be allowed to hurt us without consequence while we turn the other cheek and invite further abuse? How does the concept of grace apply to our forgiving those who wrong us?

The Freedom of Forgiveness

One noted pastor claims that the vast majority of counseling situations he encounters deal with the issue of forgiveness—either receiving it or extending it to others. "The typical counselee's most troublesome problems would be significantly diminished (and in some cases solved completely) by a right understanding of what Scripture says about forgiveness."[1]

I couldn't agree more. Unforgiveness is a deadly toxin that poisons marriages, families, friendships, and entire congregations. That realization prompted the writer of Hebrews to exhort, "See to it that no one comes short of the grace of God; that no root of bitterness springing up causes trouble, and by it many be defiled" (Hebrews 12:15).

Sooner or later, someone is going to hurt you deeply. Although you cannot control the offenses that come into your life, you do have a choice about how you will respond to those offenses. You can let go of that offense and allow the grace of God to act as a healing balm to soothe the pain. Or you can hold on to that offense, reliving the experience over and over again until it metastasizes into a tumor of bitterness and destroys your life.

The word *resentment* means "to feel again." Those who refuse to forgive choose to relive their painful experiences repeatedly. Amazingly, they have deluded themselves into thinking that by doing so, they are inflicting great harm on their offender, while in reality the offender feels none of the victim's pain. Someone has said that refusing to forgive is like drinking rat poison and then waiting for the rat to die.

It was out of my conviction that forgiveness is so crucial for our spiritual, emotional, and even physical health that I wrote a book on the topic a few years ago—*When Forgiveness Doesn't Make Sense.* In my research for the book, I worked with the Barna Research Group to conduct a national survey on Americans' attitudes about forgiveness. While you might expect that non-Christians do not have a biblical understanding of forgiveness, we were surprised to discover that only 25 percent of those who call themselves born-again Christians embrace a biblical view of forgiveness. Instead, the vast majority of Christians have accepted at least three of five common myths about forgiveness that prevent so many people from experiencing the freedom that comes from letting go of offenses:

1. Forgiveness can only be granted to those who remorsefully ask for it.
2. Forgiveness releases our offender of any consequences.
3. Forgiveness requires rebuilding a relationship with our offender.
4. Forgiveness means forgetting our offender's actions.
5. Forgiveness should be withheld in some extreme situations.[2]

Instead of rehashing the material in my book, allow me to point out how a proper understanding of grace affects our relationship with those who wrong us on a personal level.

Good Grace Forgiveness

Good Grace Affirms the Necessity of Forgiveness

Let's be clear about this: Forgiveness is not optional; it is essential for every genuine believer. In the New Testament, both Jesus and the apostle Paul spoke of the inseparable link between receiving God's forgiveness and granting forgiveness to others.

> If you do not forgive others, then your Father will not forgive your transgressions. (Matthew 6:15)

> Be kind to one another, tender-hearted, forgiving each another, *just* as God in Christ also has forgiven you. (Ephesians 4:32)

Debbie, Laura's small-group leader, had reminded Laura of the central passage in the New Testament concerning forgiveness. The point of Jesus's parable in Matthew 18 is that forgiveness is the obligation of those who have been forgiven. The first servant owed the king a debt he could never repay in a thousand lifetimes. The king, realizing the impossibility of ever receiving complete restitution from the servant, chose instead to release his servant of his obligation.

Obviously, this is a picture of our relationship to God. Our sins against our Master have created an incalculable debt. Just as the slave who could not repay his debt deserved to be thrown into prison until his obligation was satisfied, so we deserve to be cast into hell until our sin debt is paid—

which means forever. But God, like the king in the story, looks down with mercy on those who admit their need and offers to pay the debt Himself. That is grace.

Unfortunately the forgiven slave did not understand his obligation to forgive his fellow slave of the debt owed him. Sure, he had a legal right to demand repayment of the approximately sixteen dollars his fellow slave owed him, but he had no moral right to insist on repayment, given the fact that the king had just released him from a five-billion-dollar obligation!

In the same way, Jesus said that although others owe us for the hurt they have inflicted on us, we have no moral right to demand repayment, given the tremendous debt from which God has released us. The difference between how much someone else has wronged us and how much we have wronged our Master is the difference between sixteen dollars and five billion dollars! Forgiveness is the obligation of those who have been forgiven. One reason many people find it difficult to let their offenders off the hook is that they really don't understand the magnitude of the debt from which God has released them.

But another reason we struggle with forgiveness is because we have a faulty understanding of what forgiveness is…and what it is not.

Good Grace Recognizes That Forgiveness Does Not Erase the Consequences of Offenses

In his spare time Dave Hagler umpires for a recreational baseball league. One day he was stopped by a police officer for speeding. He did his best to talk the officer out of a ticket, explaining that he was usually careful and pointing out how much the ticket would raise his insurance premium. "If you don't like it, take it up with the courts," the officer said.

Next season, Hagler was umpiring the first game when the first batter approached the plate. It was the police officer who had given him a ticket.

When the officer recognized Dave, he paused a long moment before asking, "By the way, how did the thing with the ticket go?"

Hagler replied, "You'd better swing at everything."[3]

Revenge is sweet, even if it is short-lived. However, when we forgive someone, we are surrendering our right to seek revenge. The word *forgive* literally means "to release, to let go of." Simply put, forgiveness is letting go of my right to hurt you for hurting me.

In the New Testament the word *forgiveness* was used primarily to describe the release of someone from a financial obligation, such as the forgiven slave in Jesus's parable. Forgiveness does not deny the existence of a debt, nor does it allow the debt to remain unpaid. The slave owed the king a very real debt. Someone had to pay the debt in order to balance the books. But the king, realizing his slave did not have the resources to satisfy the obligation, chose to absorb the loss himself.

When God forgives us, He does not simply overlook our debt. In God's economy someone must pay for our sin. But "because of His great love with which He loved us" (Ephesians 2:4), God chose to pay the debt Himself through the death of His Son.

When someone wrongs you, the offense creates a very real obligation to you. Before you can ever release the person from the offense, you must acknowledge that there has been an offense. Then you might calculate exactly what your offender "owes" you for the wrong committed against you. Your offender may deserve divorce, the dissolution of your friendship, or even death for the pain he or she inflicted upon you. Only after you have admitted that a wrong has occurred and calculated the debt you are "owed" can you release your offender of any obligation to you.

However, you have no ability or right to release the person from the consequences other people—or even God—may require for his or her offense. Stephen, the first martyr in the New Testament, voiced his forgiveness for those who stoned him.

Then falling on his knees, he cried out with a loud voice, "Lord, do not hold this sin against them!" Having said this, he fell asleep. (Acts 7:60)

However, Stephen's forgiveness of his killers did not negate the punishment God would exact from them for their actions.

By forgiving Janet, Laura surrendered her right to sue Janet for repayment of the stolen funds. She also gave up her right to seek revenge by inflicting emotional pain on her friend by slandering her or constantly reminding her of the offense. However, Laura is powerless to remove the guilt Janet may feel toward God, to alleviate the wrath Janet might experience from her husband, or to prevent any legal action the bank may choose to take against her.

In the Bible there is a difference between seeking vengeance and seeking justice. Vengeance is the desire to make others suffer for the wrongs they have committed against us. Justice, however, is the payment that God or others (like an irate husband or an unforgiving bank) might seek from our offender. While we are to always surrender our desire for vengeance, we are never to surrender our desire for justice.

An incident in the life of King David illustrates the difference between desiring vengeance and desiring justice. Toward the end of his reign, David was constantly attacked by a man named Shimei who hurled both verbal and literal stones at David. He was the Ernest T. Bass of Israel (for those of you who are fans of *The Andy Griffith Show*). Shimei taunted David for all of his past failures, such as the Bathsheba fiasco and the rebellion of David's son Absalom.

Perhaps you have your own Shimei who delights in repeatedly reminding you of your failures. Most of us are powerless to silence our critics, but David wasn't. With a single command he could have ordered Shimei's execution with no questions asked. In fact, David's friend Abishai offered to take care of the matter by separating Shimei's head from the rest of his body.

But David refused to seek vengeance. He viewed Shimei's attacks as part of God's plan for his life. "Let him alone and let him curse, for the LORD has told him," David concluded (2 Samuel 16:11). "Perhaps those verbal bricks Shimei continues to fling at me will remind me of the pain that comes from disobedience," the disgraced king reasoned to himself.

However, on his deathbed David instructed his son Solomon to execute Shimei. Why the change of heart? Was the king suddenly overtaken by bitterness? Was this his last attempt to settle the score? Not at all.

David realized that a blasphemer like Shimei who repeatedly cursed God (and others) would do irreparable harm to the kingdom. While David could surrender his right to vengeance, he could not relinquish the obligation he had for the welfare of the nation. David's position of authority required him to deal with the sin of Shimei. But significantly, David allowed someone else to take care of exacting justice from his tormentor.

Forgiveness means surrendering our right to get even for personal offenses. However, we cannot absolve our offender of the consequences he or she may face from others or from God.

Good Grace Understands That Although Forgiveness Can Be Granted, Reconciliation Must Be Earned

The most pervasive myth about forgiveness is that we can only offer it to those who ask for it. The argument is that since God only forgives those who request His forgiveness, we can only forgive those who repent of having wronged us. But that line of reasoning fails to distinguish between receiving forgiveness and granting forgiveness. I can only receive forgiveness from God or others if I ask for it. But I can grant forgiveness to someone even if the person is unwilling or unable to request it.

Jesus described the kind of unconditional forgiveness we should extend to others:

> Whenever you stand praying, forgive, if you have anything
> against anyone, so that your Father who is in heaven will also
> forgive you your transgressions. But if you do not forgive, neither
> will your Father who is in heaven forgive your transgressions.
> (Mark 11:25-26)

Imagine that you're sitting in church one Sunday morning, and your pastor leads the congregation in a time of silent meditation. Suddenly you recall a harsh remark your boss spoke to you last week, a betrayal by a former mate years ago, or sexual abuse by a relative that you endured as a child. What are you suppose to do? "Forgive them," Jesus says. "But Lord, how can I forgive since…

"My boss is not here today to confess his insensitivity."

"I've lost track of my former mate."

"My abusive family member is dead."

Jesus says that we possess the power to unilaterally forgive our offender. We do not have to depend on someone else's actions to experience the physical, emotional, and spiritual healing that comes from forgiving that person. When we forgive someone, we are saying, "What that person did to me was wrong. He has hurt me deeply and deserves to pay for his offense. But today I am releasing him of the obligation he has toward me. I am not forgiving him because he has asked to be forgiven or deserves to be forgiven. I am forgiving him because of the tremendous forgiveness God has offered me."

However, beyond the spiritual obligation we have to forgive, there is a practical benefit to unconditional, unilateral forgiveness. When I was in high school, my best friend and I saw the movie *The Thing with Two Heads*, starring Ray Milland and Rosey Grier. This quintessential B movie was about a man with two heads, played by Milland and Grier wearing a ridiculous-looking costume. Grier was the "evil head" always tormenting the "good head" played by Milland. One can hardly imagine a worse fate than spending your life joined to someone who taunts you 24/7.

But that is exactly what happens when we refuse to forgive another person. We emotionally bond ourselves to our offender. He or she is right there with us, repeatedly inflicting the same hurt as we choose to continually relive the experience. In his book *None of These Diseases*, Dr. S. I. McMillen wrote,

> The man I hate hounds me wherever I go. I can't escape his tyranni-
> cal grasp on my mind. When the waiter serves me porterhouse steak
> with French fries, asparagus, crisp salad, and strawberry shortcake
> smothered with ice cream, it might as well be stale bread and water.
> My teeth chew the food and I swallow it, but the man I hate will
> not permit me to enjoy it.[4]

When I forgive someone, I am severing the emotional bond that ties me to the person who has wronged me. Since I am no longer expecting anything from my offender, I am free to get on with my life.

Robin Casarjian, a secular psychotherapist, observed,

> So often when people think about forgiveness they think about
> what it's going to do for someone else.... What they don't realize is
> that forgiveness is really an act of self-interest. We're doing ourselves
> a favor because we become free to have a more peaceful life—we
> free ourselves from being emotional victims of others.[5]

Although unconditional forgiveness is both possible and profitable, it does not always result in reconciliation with our offender. I may forgive a cheating mate, but I may not choose to continue the marriage. I may forgive a friend who has betrayed me, but I may also choose to change the nature of our relationship. I may forgive the parent who constantly belittles me, but I may choose not to visit or call as often.

Bad grace insists that forgiveness always results in restoring a relationship to its "preoffense" condition. But good grace recognizes that such restoration is not always possible. Why? Although forgiveness is unconditional, reconciliation depends on several conditions.

Let's return to Laura and Janet's story for a moment. Although Laura is willing to forgive Janet for the stolen money, Janet's actions have created a rift in their friendship. Before that fissure can be closed, Janet must first demonstrate genuine *repentance* by admitting her wrongdoing and making a commitment not to repeat the offense. While repentance on the part of our offender is never a requirement for forgiveness, it is essential for reconciliation. Until our offender admits the wrong and demonstrates a willingness to change, there can never be complete reconciliation.

Isn't that true in our relationship with God? Although we may have received forgiveness for our sins through our faith in Christ, it is still possible for us to injure our relationship with God through our disobedience. It is not that God moves away from us when we sin. We move away from Him. The prophet Amos used that word picture when he posed a simple question to the Israelites: "Can two walk together, except they be agreed?" (Amos 3:3, KJV).

For two people to walk together, they have to agree on their direction and their ultimate destination. The moment one party starts acting independently of the other, their walk together is effectively over.

The Israelites in Amos's day had changed directions. They had chosen to move away from God and pursue a different destination. Because they were living apart from God, they were no longer in a position to experience His blessings. The only remedy that could restore their fractured relationship with Yahweh was turning around and heading in a new direction. The future of their relationship depended upon *their* willingness, not God's, to change directions (the meaning of the word *repent*).

The same truth applies in our relationship to other people. If you have been wronged by a friend, but that friend maintains his or her innocence, it will be difficult to continue your relationship—at least at the level you once enjoyed. You are not in agreement with each other on a very substantive issue: how you have been treated. Until the other person admits having wronged you, you will find it difficult to "walk together." Fortunately, Janet admitted her mistake and asked for Laura's forgiveness.

However, repentance alone is not always sufficient for the restoration of a broken relationship. Many times reconciliation demands *restitution* on the part of our offender. While Laura may decide to preserve her friendship with Janet, whether or not she chooses to remain in business with her may depend on Janet's willingness to repay the fifteen hundred dollars she stole from their joint checking account.

Desiring restitution and seeking revenge should never be confused. Revenge is my desire to make my offender suffer for his or her offense. Restitution is my offender's desire to make repayment for the wrong he or she committed against me.

Remember the story of Zaccheus, the tax collector who had cheated so many people out of so much money? Once he met Jesus and received forgiveness, Zaccheus volunteered to repay those he had cheated, offering up to four times the amount he had stolen (see Luke 19:8-9). His restitution was evidence of the sincerity of his desire for reconciliation with both God and his fellow Jews.

Finally, reconciliation with someone who has wronged us requires the *rebuilding* of fractured trust. A wife who has been physically abused by her husband can and should forgive her mate—for her own benefit. But she does not have to continue living in such an abusive relationship that endangers her life or the lives of her children. The belief in the sanctity of human life applies not only to fetuses inside the womb but also to those outside the womb! Since our bodies are God's creation, we should treat them with honor and not subject them to unnecessary violence. To do so would be an affront to the God who created us and breathed into us the precious gift of life.

Some might ask, "But what about Jesus's command to 'turn the other cheek' when someone slaps us?" In Jesus's day slapping someone on the cheek was a sign of contempt and did not pose a serious safety threat. So Jesus was saying that when someone insults us, we are not to seek revenge.

Before an abused wife agrees to live with her husband again, she would want to see evidence of his genuine repentance. She would want to know that he has undergone a process of rehabilitation for his violent outbursts through spiritual counseling and accountability with other men. All of that takes time. A relationship can be broken in just a few seconds through a violent outburst, a careless statement, or an unwise decision, but it may take months if not years to rebuild trust.

In Janet and Laura's situation, neither their friendship nor their business relationship can be restored instantly. Healing takes time. The one who has broken the relationship is in no position to demand the immediate restoration of the relationship. He or she can only request forgiveness and then wait for the wounded party to heal.

Bad grace equates forgiveness with reconciliation.

Bad grace underestimates the serious and long-lasting consequences of sin.

Bad grace places all of the burden on the offended party and little on the offender.

On the other hand…

Good grace understands that forgiveness depends on me, but reconciliation depends on us.

Good grace teaches that forgiveness "has no strings attached," but reconciliation has "several strings attached."[6]

Good grace recognizes that although reconciliation is always preferable, it is not always possible.

CHAPTER SEVEN

Good Grace Marriages

The other day I was visiting with a publisher friend and asked the question every writer worth his salt asks after the obligatory pleasantries are out of the way: "What's selling well these days?"

Without hesitation he answered, "Anything having to do with the family."

I sighed because I have not yet been able to summon the willpower to write my "family" book. One reason is that my children are adolescents, and I figure it's not safe for me to offer any advice until they are both grown and out of the house and have several children of their own.

But the main reason I find it difficult to write a book on the family is that…well…everything has already been said that needs to be said. For the past fifty years, biblical teachings about the family have received more print space and airtime than all other doctrines of the faith combined. If you don't believe that, visit your local Christian bookstore and compare the shelf space devoted to marriage and parenting books to the amount of space devoted to theology books. Or tune in to your local Christian radio station and note how many programs deal with issues related to home life. How well do you think a radio program titled "Focus on Soteriology" would do in the ratings?

I am not at all begrudging this emphasis on the family. After all, home is where we live. As a husband and father I appreciate any and all the help I can get in maintaining and improving life's most important relationships. Nevertheless, one has to wonder how much benefit families are deriving from this flood of information.

Apparently, not much. Consider the dismal statistics concerning Christian marriages. A recent study conducted by The Barna Group found that "among married born again Christians, 35% have experienced a divorce. That figure is identical to the outcome among married adults who are not born again."[1]

Obviously, something is wrong with this picture! Why is it that those who have received—and actually claim to believe—God's instructions for marriage as revealed in the Bible brazenly ignore those same instructions? Two words: bad grace.

We tend to view the biblical instructions concerning marriage the same way we view a car manufacturer's instructions for achieving optimum gas mileage—nice if you choose to follow them, but not absolutely necessary. Sure, if you keep your tires properly inflated, refuse to drive over 70 mph, and use a better grade of fuel, you may add a mile or two per gallon. But if you don't, no big deal. In fact, the only people who are fanatical about following such suggestions are nerdy men who carry plastic pocket protectors and tire gauges in their shirt pockets.

In the same way, bad grace treats the biblical mandates for marriage more as suggestions than commands. In an ideal world Christians would only marry Christians, couples would remain faithful to each other for an entire lifetime, and divorce would be out of the question. However, since we don't live in the Garden of Eden, we are incapable of always meeting God's standard—or so we are led to believe.

Not to worry, though, because grace covers a multitude of mistakes, including those made in marriage. We think of grace as a magic wand we can wave over disobedience, and expect the pain that always accompanies affairs, spiritually mixed marriages, and divorce to instantly disappear. If that is true, no wonder Christians are so cavalier in their disregard for God's instructions about marriage.

But a proper understanding of good grace recognizes that while grace eradicates the wall of separation that sin erects between God and us, it does not erase the short-term consequences of our disobedience. When I was a little boy, I decided one night that I did not want to go to bed as my parents had instructed. So I stood in my baby bed and screamed at the top of my lungs (great preparation for becoming a Baptist preacher). Several times my parents came in and asked me to be quiet and go to sleep. Realizing I was not getting sufficient attention, I jumped over the railing, fell on the floor, and broke my arm. Of course, my parents forgave me this small-scale rebellion. Nevertheless, I had to deal with the consequences of a broken arm.

Good grace recognizes that while every violation of our Father's commands is forgivable, those violations result in negative consequences that we must deal with.

God reminded the Israelites of this truth:

See, I am setting before you today a blessing and a curse: the blessing, if you listen to the commandments of the LORD your God, which I am commanding you today; and the curse, if you do not listen. (Deuteronomy 11:26-28)

Nowhere is the link between our obedience and God's blessing (and the corollary, our disobedience and God's curse) felt more acutely than in the marriage relationship. Emotional separation, sexual dissatisfaction, and tragic divorces are just some of the undesirable by-products of ignoring God's instructions for marriage.

However, the proponents of bad grace attempt to sweep those consequences under the rug. Grace, they promise, is a balm that is guaranteed to remove the sting of disobedience. Specifically, "bad gracers" promote three lies regarding the formation, fidelity, and finality of marriage. (I will expose the first two lies in this chapter and the third lie in chapter 8.) These lies are responsible for the distance, dissatisfaction, and divorce that plague so many marriages today.

Lie No. 1: "Grace Means I Can Marry Whomever I Want"

Whenever I am asked to speak to a group of high-school or college students, I usually know what topic to address without much soul searching. "How to Find a Mate" is a guaranteed crowd pleaser. Of the thousands of potential life partners in your world, how can you be expected to discover the "right" one for you?

In my talk I use the story in Genesis 24 that recounts Abraham's efforts to secure a bride for his son. The old patriarch dispatched his chief servant to find a mate for Isaac. I explain to the crowd that in the Middle Eastern culture, marriages were (and still are in many cases) arranged by the parents. The students' reaction to this bit of cultural information is predictable: "You've got to be kidding! I would rather go through life single than have my parents choose my mate!"

Westerners pride themselves on individualism that encourages us to make our own choices in life, including the choice of whom to marry. But could that freedom be more of a curse than a blessing? If our choice of a mate is based on mutual physical and emotional attraction, what happens when that attraction diminishes due to the passing of time?

In an arranged marriage, the union between a man and woman is founded not upon mutual attraction but on the agreement of others. As one writer notes, "Having heard your parents' decision, you accept that you will live for many years with someone you now barely know. Thus the over-riding question changes from 'Whom should I marry?' to 'Given this part-ner, what kind of marriage can we construct together?'"[2]

I am not advocating that we adopt the practice of arranged marriages (although it's hard to imagine that it could be any more prone to failure than our current system), but I do think it would be helpful to remember that we are not free to marry whomever we choose. Our heavenly Father has narrowed the field of available mates by insisting on two guidelines we must follow if we want to experience His blessings in our marriage.

First, *our mate must be a member of the opposite sex*. Go ahead and say what my teenage daughter occasionally feels compelled to say, "Thank you, Captain Obvious!" Until recently, such a natural boundary would not have needed to be mentioned. But the government's increasing recognition of same-sex "marriages" makes it necessary for us to reiterate the truth that marriage is only for a male and female.

Amazingly, the drive to legitimize homosexual unions is finding increas-ing support among members of mainline denominations. The promotion several years ago of a homosexual bishop who left his wife and two young children for another man is just one example of the seismic cultural shift in attitudes toward homosexuality, even among professing Christians.

Some would say that while marriage to a member of the opposite sex is preferable for the continuance of the species, it is not always possible. Because of either sociological or genetic factors, some people are naturally attracted to members of the same sex. Should these people be denied the fulfillment that comes from a loving, monogamous union? Shouldn't God's grace cover the biological or sociological disorder that has led to their condition?

Recent efforts by conservative politicians to enact a constitutional amendment defining marriage as a relationship between a man and a woman have been denounced by gay activists. In a statement regarding

President Bush's attempt to restrict governmental recognition of marriage to a relationship between a man and a woman, the political director of the nation's largest gay-rights organization, Human Rights Campaign, said, "We are very disappointed that the president is trying to further codify discrimination into law."[3]

But looking to the electorate or judiciary to define marriage is necessary only for those who refuse to accept the Bible as God's authoritative Word on the subject. Before it ever became a plank in a political party's platform, God gave his own definition of what constitutes a legitimate marriage. Jesus reaffirmed this principle when answering the Pharisees' questions about divorce (which we will examine later):

> Have you not read that He who created them from the beginning
> made them male and female, and said, "For this reason a man shall
> leave his father and mother and be joined to his wife, and the two
> shall become one flesh"? (Matthew 19:4-5)

Without resorting to the usual evangelical clichés, such as "In the beginning God created Adam and Eve, not Adam and Steve," it is worth noting that God's original design for marriage involved the coming together of two people who complemented rather than duplicated each other. Originally God promised to provide Adam with a helper who was "suitable for him" (Genesis 2:18). The Hebrew word translated "suitable" means "opposite." God designed marriage to be the union of two individuals who are diverse in their emotional as well as their sexual makeup. John Piper explains why such a union is to be celebrated:

> By creating a person *like* Adam yet very *unlike* Adam, God provided
> the possibility of a profound unity that would otherwise have been
> impossible. A different kind of unity is enjoyed by the joining of

diverse counterparts than is enjoyed by joining two things just alike. When we all sing the same melody line it is called "unison," which means "one sound." But when we unite diverse lines of soprano and alto and tenor and bass, we call it harmony, and everyone who has an ear to hear knows that something is touched in us more deeply by great harmony than by unison. So God made a woman and not another man. He created heterosexuality, not homosexuality. God's first institution was marriage, not the fraternity.[4]

The second guideline we must follow if we want to experience God's blessings in our marriage is that *our mate must be a believer.* In both the Old and New Testaments, God's Word is clear: Believers are only to marry other believers. As the Israelites prepared to enter the Promised Land in Canaan, God knew that they would be tempted to marry the Canaanites who were already residing in the land. The problem with the Canaanites was not their race but their god. Because they worshiped Baal, God warned,

> You shall not intermarry with them; you shall not give your daugh-
> ters to their sons, nor shall you take their daughters for your sons.
> For they will turn your sons away from following Me to serve other
> gods; then the anger of the LORD will be kindled against you and
> He will quickly destroy you. (Deuteronomy 7:3-4)

The primary reason God gives for not marrying an unbeliever is the spiritual devastation such an unequal union produces in the life of the believer. While in some rare cases, the believing mate may positively influence the unbelieving spouse, the reverse is far more common: The unbeliever hinders the believer's relationship with God. As a pastor I see this principle at work all too often. For every case in which the believing spouse leads the unbelieving spouse to Christ, I can cite a dozen cases in which the unbelieving mate so harasses, berates, or discourages the Christian that he or she finally stops attending a Bible-believing congregation, supporting God's work financially, or trying to exert a spiritual influence on the children, all in a futile attempt to maintain peace in the home.

Some would protest, "But Robert, you're quoting from the Old Testament law. We live under grace, not law." In the New Testament the apostle Paul restated the same principle that believers are only to marry other believers:

> Do not be bound together with unbelievers; for what partnership
> have righteousness and lawlessness, or what fellowship has light with
> darkness? (2 Corinthians 6:14)

In addition to damaging our relationship with God, marriage to an unbeliever also disrupts our relationship with our mate. The phrase translated "bound together" pictures two unequal animals, such as an ox and a donkey, being harnessed together to perform a task. In such an arrangement, the ox will pull against the donkey, and the donkey will work against the ox, resulting in constant friction and eventual stalemate.

A Christian and non-Christian are similarly mismatched in marriage. How can you join a believer and unbeliever together in the marriage "harness" and expect them to work together? They will continually pull against each other. Their different value systems will result in radically different philosophies about finances, sex, life goals, and parenting. Such differences will produce constant conflict unless one party chooses to compromise his or her belief system to keep the peace. Spiritual opposites do not attract each other; they end up attacking each other.

Bob grew up in a non-Christian home, but during a brief stint in the air force, he was led to Christ by a chaplain. After concluding his military service, Bob met Judy, a smart, vivacious girl to whom he was instantly attracted. Although Judy came from a religious home, she had never developed a personal relationship with Christ. Of course, this greatly disturbed Bob, who would take her with him to church services and Bible studies. But she remained unconvinced and unconverted. In spite of their spiritual differences, Bob married Judy, praying that one day she would become a Christian.

A few years after their marriage, the world-famous evangelist Billy Graham conducted a crusade in their city. Bob persuaded Judy to accompany him to the service that was being held in the local football stadium. Judy, now pregnant with their first child, acquiesced to her husband's request, and at the crusade she became a Christian. The following Sunday she voluntarily accompanied Bob to his church and made her decision public and was later baptized.

Judy immersed herself (pardon the pun) in the Bible and became a premier Bible teacher in that congregation. She used her role as a public school teacher as a platform to share her faith and led hundreds of her students to Christ. Their first child became a pastor, their second child became a deacon in his church, and their third child married a pastor. And it all started with a husband who desired to lead his wife to faith in Christ.

Now here is the question: Given the numerous commands in both the Old and New Testaments for Christians only to marry other Christians, was it wrong for Bob to marry Judy? Did grace give Bob a free pass to violate God's instructions, especially since he was a new Christian and did not know what the Bible taught about marriage? Doesn't the positive outcome prove that we should not be rigid about God's boundaries for choosing a mate?

Yes, no, and no. Yes, it was wrong for Bob to have married Judy. No, grace did not excuse Bob's disobedience. And no, the positive outcome does not justify disregarding God's boundaries. Before you accuse me of being overly harsh, you should know that Bob and Judy were my parents, who are now in heaven. In saying they should not have married (at least while my mother was not a Christian), I realize I am arguing against my own existence, since I would not be sitting at a keyboard typing these words had these two individuals not come together when they did!

Yet what kind of marriage would my parents have experienced if my father had waited to marry my mother until after she had become a Christian? Sure, the story had a good ending, but how much better could it have been? Someone has said that success is measured not by the way things are but by the way things are compared to how they could be.

Of course, God's will is large enough to encompass the fall of Lucifer, the rebellion of Adam and Eve, the crucifixion of Jesus Christ, and even the disobedience of my parents. In some mysterious way, God is able to cause all things—even evil things—to work together for His purpose. Nevertheless, grace does not provide us with carte blanche to violate God's boundaries in choosing a mate.

Lie No. 2: "I Can Cheat Without Lasting Consequences"

The other night my two daughters and I were in our den, each of us working on our own projects. "What are you doing?" I asked my younger daughter. She explained that she was writing a report on a well-known political leader.

"You know that he had a lot of affairs with other women even though he was married, don't you?" I said. I'm not sure why I felt compelled to share this tidbit of information that I was sure had been omitted from my daughter's history book. Although she was disheartened at the news, my older daughter was indignant.

"Dad, he was a Christian. His sins aren't any worse than your sins. You shouldn't be so judgmental." Spoken like a true sixteen-year-old—and many Christians today. How many times have you heard the following statements?

"God doesn't grade sin."

"No sin is worse than any other sin."

"God condemns gossip as much as He condemns adultery."

Usually such pronouncements about the equality of sin are spoken in the context of sexual immorality, the inference being that the Christian community's harsh attitude toward sins of the flesh is symptomatic of some Freudian hang-up that says more about the accuser than about the accused. One writer observes, "I dwell on the church's severe attitude toward sex because I believe we Christians bear heavy responsibility for the counter-reaction so evident in modern society.... How is it that we who follow him [Jesus] use the word 'immoral' to signify sexual sins almost exclusively and reserve church discipline for those who fail sexually?"[5]

Such declarations, while containing a measure of truth, give the impression that sexual sins are no different from any other sins. Furthermore, because of grace, people who cheat on their mates and repent are forever free of any emotional or physical consequences for their transgressions—or so we are led to believe.

But the Bible, not to mention everyday experience, tells us differently. Yes, Christ's death on the cross has resulted in the forgiveness of "all our transgressions" (Colossians 2:13), but some acts of disobedience result in more severe consequences than others—at least in this life. For example, in God's eyes, hating someone is tantamount to killing that person. But no one ever fried in the electric chair for harboring harsh feelings toward another human being. While God's forgiveness ensures that a repentant killer will never have to face God's judgment, it does not exempt him or her from facing man's justice.

The same principle applies in the arena of sexual immorality. The married woman who notices a cute guy at the gym and secretly fantasizes about him is just as guilty of impurity in God's eyes as the pastor who carries on a torrid affair with his secretary. While both can be forgiven by God, the pastor faces more potentially damaging consequences for his actions. Sexually transmitted diseases, divorce, and dismissal from jobs or leadership positions in a church are just some of the consequences of adulterous relationships.

Consider King David's experience. His adulterous relationship with Bathsheba is well known. One spring evening, when love and lust filled the air, David decided that God's rules did not apply to him—at least not that night. He summoned Bathsheba to his bedroom, and the rest, as they say, is history. But when David's immorality and subsequent cover-up were exposed, David asked for and received God's forgiveness. His plea for mercy is recorded in one of the best-loved psalms in Scripture:

> Be gracious to me, O God, according to Your lovingkindness;
> According to the greatness of Your compassion blot out my
>   transgressions.
> Wash me thoroughly from my iniquity
> And cleanse me from my sin. (Psalm 51:1-2)

David received the forgiveness for which he prayed. In a companion psalm, he exclaimed,

> How blessed is he whose transgression is forgiven,
> Whose sin is covered!
> How blessed is the man to whom the LORD does not impute
>   iniquity. (Psalm 32:1-2)

David was expressing the exhilaration that comes from realizing we never need to dread the prospect that God will dredge up some past mistake and say, "Remember when you…?" Grace means that our sins are forgiven…forgotten…forever.

Nevertheless, David spent many years experiencing the consequences of his actions. A dead child, a dishonored reputation, a disobedient son, and a divided kingdom—all of which God linked to David's adulterous relationship with Bathsheba—were part of his life until the day he died. Now here's another insight from Captain Obvious: Had David gone no further than fantasizing about Bathsheba, he never would have experienced any of these consequences. Yes, some sins *are* worse than others in terms of their consequences.

Bad grace, when applied to sexual immorality, will always downplay the effects of sin. Bad gracers give the impression, whether intentional or not, that when God forgives a Christian of adultery, He is somehow obligated to rebuild fractured marriages, heal sexually transmitted diseases, and restore severely damaged reputations. When that doesn't happen, people become disillusioned with their faith and wonder, "What use is God's grace if I must still suffer the consequences of my actions?"

By contrast, good grace brings about righteous and life-enriching results.

Good Grace Satisfies God's Desires Concerning Forgiveness

Good grace never shies away from affirming God's willingness and ability to forgive any sin, including adultery. However, good grace also recognizes a simple but often-overlooked truth: God's forgiveness is only available to those who ask for it. And those who ask for it must do so with a repentant heart. The essence of the word *repentance,* as we saw in chapter 4, is a turning away from sin. Without that kind of heartfelt contrition, there can be no forgiveness.

The sacrifices of God are a broken spirit;
A broken and a contrite heart, O God, You will not despise.
(Psalm 51:17)

Doug, a professing Christian, had been involved in a long-term affair with his best friend's wife, Sherrie. Although he was unwilling to end the affair, occasional pangs of guilt caused Doug to confide in his pastor about his situation. "Pastor, do you think God will forgive me for this affair?"

The pastor turned to Matthew 18:8-9 and asked Doug to read it aloud:

If your hand or your foot causes you to stumble, cut it off and
throw it from you; it is better for you to enter life crippled or lame,
than to have two hands or two feet and be cast into the eternal fire.
If your eye causes you to stumble, pluck it out and throw it from
you. It is better for you to enter life with one eye, than to have two
eyes and be cast into the fiery hell.

"Doug, Jesus says that unless you are willing to resist this relationship with every ounce of strength you have, *you have no hope of going to heaven.*" While such a statement seems extreme, so do Jesus's words about removing body parts! Good grace refuses to offer any assurance of forgiveness to those who are unwilling to turn away from their sin. Although our repentance does not earn God's grace, it affirms that we have received it.

Good Grace Emphasizes the Harmful Consequences of Disobedience

While bad grace minimizes the consequences of sin, good grace underscores them—just as the Bible does. King Solomon was one of the by-products of David's adulterous relationship with Bathsheba after the first child died. Solomon witnessed firsthand the lingering effects of immoral relationships in his father's life. Perhaps that is what led Solomon to offer this counsel concerning adultery:

The one who commits adultery with a woman is lacking sense;

He who would destroy himself does it.

Wounds and disgrace he will find,

And his reproach will not be blotted out. (Proverbs 6:32-33)

Although in God's eyes, David's sin was blotted out (see Psalm 51:1), other people in David's life had better memories than God! David's disgrace followed him the rest of his life.

A number of years ago, Chuck Swindoll listed in his weekly church newsletter some of the practical consequences of adulterous relationships, even those that have been confessed and forgiven. Here's a sampling from the list:

- "Your mate will immediately be isolated by most of those who once stood near. Guilt, shame and rejection he or she is sure to feel will accompany the anguish of loneliness.
- "The total devastation it will bring to your children. Their growth, innocence, trust and healthy outlook on life will be permanently damaged.
- "The heartache you will cause to your parents, your family, your peers, your mentors and your disciples will be indescribable.
- "You will never be able to erase the fall from your (or others') mind.... This will remain indelibly etched on your life's record.
- "Your escapade(s) will introduce to your life and your mate's life the very real probability of a sexually transmitted disease.
- "The name of Jesus Christ, whom you once honored, will be tarnished, giving the enemies of faith further reason to sneer and jeer."

Chuck then concludes with these words. "Solomon was right. 'The way of the transgressor is *hard.*' Forgiveness may come. The affair(s) may end. Restoration to fellowship may occur. But these consequences will not go away."[6]

Good Grace Affirms the Benefits of Forgiveness

Imagine that a co-worker said to you, "I'm thinking about stealing five thousand dollars from our company. What do you think?"

Would you say, "God loves you and will forgive you even if you steal the money"?

More likely, you would emphasize the risks involved with embezzlement, such as the loss of employment, possible imprisonment, and a tarnished reputation.

On the other hand, suppose you were visiting your co-worker in jail after he had already been convicted of the crime. Hopefully, you would assure him of God's willingness to forgive him and help him visualize a new life once he is released from jail.

How much we should emphasize God's grace depends on whether we are on the front end or back end of sin. The previous list I cited of horrible consequences that often accompany adulterous relationships would be appropriate to give someone who is either contemplating an affair or is involved in one. But someone who has turned away from an adulterous relationship needs to be reminded of God's grace.

"But what good is grace if I still must spend a lifetime suffering the results of my mistake?" someone might wonder.

First, grace means you don't have to spend all of eternity suffering for your mistake. Thirty years beats thirty billion years! But even the relatively short-term discomfort we experience for our disobedience is in itself evidence of God's love. The pain of a fractured marriage that may take years to heal, the loss of a job, and the humiliation we experience with friends and family members all have a way of reminding us of the seriousness of sin and can serve as deterrents to future disobedience.

Such an idea is not original with me. David believed that the continuing consequences he experienced for his relationship with Bathsheba served as an inoculation against future disobedience:

> Before I was afflicted I went astray,
> But now I keep Your word. (Psalm 119:67)

Bad grace infers that we can violate our marriage vows without lasting consequences. Good grace recognizes that although all sins are forgivable, the effects of adultery continue long after God has pronounced us forgiven.

Bad grace promotes a third lie about marriage that deserves a chapter of its own…

CHAPTER EIGHT

Good Grace Divorce

How would you respond to the following scenarios?

- You are a member of a large church with a well-known pastor who is a television preacher. One Sunday morning he tearfully announces to the congregation that his marriage of twenty-five years is ending due to irreconcilable differences. He assures the congregation that there is no immorality involved, but that divorce seems to be the only option. The church is divided on whether he should remain as pastor. Some argue that if his own home is in disarray, he is disqualified from serving as pastor according to 1 Timothy 3:1-5. But others say that the pastor needs grace, not judgment, during this difficult time in his life. Even if he has not been an ideal husband, who among us has a perfect marriage? Doesn't God's grace cover all our inadequacies? A church business meeting is scheduled so members can vote on whether to retain the pastor. How would you vote?
- A close friend confides to you her discovery that her husband is addicted to pornography. She has also discovered receipts in his pockets indicating that he has visited some upscale gentlemen's

clubs while on out-of-town business trips. Although there is no indication that he has slept with other women, your friend is devastated by her husband's betrayal. When she confronts him about it, he says, "I'm sorry for hurting you, but I can't help myself. I need this kind of excitement." He refuses to seek counseling and makes no promises to stop his behavior. Your friend tells you, "I don't know how I can ever allow him to touch me again. Even though he isn't technically guilty of adultery, hasn't he committed spiritual adultery by lusting after these other women? I want a divorce." What advice would you offer your friend?

• Your recently married daughter calls you in tears. "I just can't take it any longer. Ken is abusing me, and I don't want to live any longer if it means staying married to him." Alarmed, you ask if he is physically assaulting her. "No, it's worse than that. He is always berating me, telling me I'm worthless. He goes into uncontrollable fits of rage. Although he hasn't hit me yet, I'm afraid he'll eventually hurt me or even kill me. I want out of this marriage." What counsel would you provide your daughter?

Few topics cause as much controversy among Christians as the subject of divorce and remarriage. The hottest deacons' meeting I ever attended had nothing to do with church finances or great doctrinal issues, such as predestination or eschatology. It was about whether a divorced man was permitted to serve as a deacon. Some deacons argued that even if the Bible allows for divorce and remarriage, church leaders need to maintain a higher standard, given the epidemic of divorce among believers. Others countered that the church should be known as a dispenser of grace, not judgment. "Why do we insist on shooting the most wounded people in our congregation by treating divorce as the unpardonable sin?" they asked.

In the previous chapter we considered what good grace says about two common misconceptions about marriage: "I can marry whomever I want" and "I can cheat without any lasting consequences." In this chapter we are going to examine a third lie about the marriage relationship that is as prevalent within the church as it is outside the church: *"Grace allows me to divorce if I'm in an unhappy marriage."*

How does grace apply to the increasingly common experience of failed marriages? Admittedly some Christians impose an unreasonable standard that prohibits divorce and remarriage under any circumstance whatsoever. When asked about the passages in the Bible that allow for divorce and remarriage under certain circumstances, either they will reply with some tortured interpretation of the text that defies reason, or they will concede that although such "exceptions" do exist, they do not represent "God's best."

I remember hearing Pastor John MacArthur relate a conversation he had with Bill Gothard, a respected Bible teacher who advocates the "no divorce and remarriage" position. John asked Bill, "But what about the passage in Matthew 19:9 that allows for divorce in the case of infidelity?" They were walking by a chicken coop at the time, and Bill pointed to the coop and asked rhetorically, "What would happen if there were a hole in that coop? The chickens would use that one hole to escape."

Obviously, the inference was that if provided an "out" to the marriage relationship, most people would use it. John replied, "But, Bill, what if there were no chicken coop? What would Matthew 19:9 mean?"

As we have already seen, legalists add to the standards set in God's Word. "I know the Bible says this, but in today's world we need to realize that..." is their constant refrain as they equate their opinions with divine revelation. In Jesus's day such people were members of the Jewish sect known as the Pharisees that added more than six hundred additional rules to the Mosaic Law, which already included the Ten Commandments!

Jesus refused to cut them any slack. His most scathing indictments were not against adulterers, murderers, or thieves, but against legalists who "tie up heavy burdens and lay them on men's shoulders.… Woe to you, scribes and Pharisees, hypocrites, because you shut off the kingdom of heaven from people" (Matthew 23:4,13).

The Pharisees who populate today's churches are not content with the biblical guidelines for divorce and remarriage. Instead, they advocate a "no divorce for any reason" standard, in spite of what the Bible teaches. Yes, some of these passages can be interpreted differently. Nevertheless, it is clear that in at least *some* circumstances, divorce and remarriage are permissible. But the legalist refuses to allow for that, using rising divorce statistics and chicken coops as arguments for enforcing a "higher standard."

On the other hand, libertarians continually aim to lower the scriptural standard regarding divorce and remarriage. For them, grace offers a free pass to exit turbulent marriages in search of greener pastures. While divorce is never preferable, they argue, it is sometimes necessary—and not just for the reasons given in Scripture. If my mate is verbally abusive, lowers my self-esteem, has life goals incompatible with mine, differs in parenting philosophies, is a financial time bomb waiting to explode, or just makes life miserable for me, does God really expect me to spend the rest of my life with such a person? How could a loving, grace-giving God sentence me to a lifetime of misery?

A recent article in a Christian magazine featured a profile of a well-known entertainer who left her husband and the father of her children for a married man. The article concluded with these words: "At last _____ is happy." In the world of bad grace, happiness, not obedience, is the standard by which many people gauge their decisions. When it comes to the issue of divorce and remarriage, "What will make me happiest?" rather than "What will make God happiest?" is the determining factor.

But a proper understanding of grace neither raises nor lowers God's standard regarding marriage and divorce. Instead, it recognizes two important principles.

Good Grace Recognizes That Divorce and Remarriage Are Allowable in Two Specific Situations

First, Jesus taught that *adultery* provided grounds for divorce. As we saw earlier in Matthew 19, the Pharisees asked Jesus, "Is it lawful for a man to divorce his wife for any reason at all?" (verse 3). In Jesus's day the Jews were just as divided over the divorce dilemma as Christians are today. Those who followed the conservative rabbi Shammai were in the "no divorce for any reason" camp, while disciples of the more liberal teacher Hillel advocated the "divorce for any reason" philosophy. If your wife burns a bagel at breakfast, you're free to marry someone else, they taught.

The Pharisees, as always, thought they could paint Jesus into a corner and destroy His credibility by forcing Him to take sides in this explosive issue. But the Lord wisely pointed them back to the Old Testament. "You guys who are experts in the Old Testament surely know what the Scripture teaches about this," Jesus said as He reminded them of the Creation account recorded in Genesis:

> Have you not read that He who created them from the beginning made them male and female, and said, "For this reason a man shall leave his father and mother and be joined to his wife; and the two shall become one flesh"?... What therefore God has joined together, let no man separate. (verses 4-6)

The whole question about divorce and remarriage is quite simple when you understand God's original design for marriage: one man and one woman joined together in an unbreakable bond for life. Nevertheless, Jesus recognized one instance in which that bond can be broken:

> I say to you, whoever divorces his wife, except for immorality, and marries another woman commits adultery. (verse 9)

If you divorce your mate and marry another person, you are guilty of adultery, unless your mate was guilty of "immorality."

Throughout history, people have offered varying interpretations of what Jesus meant by "immorality." Some believe that Jesus was referring to unfaithfulness during the engagement or betrothal period. For example, when Joseph discovered that his fiancée, Mary, was pregnant by someone other than himself, he considered ending the relationship. (He soon learned that the "someone" was the Holy Spirit!) Thus, Jesus was saying that unfaithfulness during an engagement period is grounds for ending the relationship. However, since Jesus was answering questions about marriage, not engagement, this interpretation is improbable.

Others believe that Jesus was referring to "immoral marriages," such as incestuous or homosexual unions. But since the Old Testament already condemned such arrangements, that interpretation is also suspect.

The traditional interpretation of this passage is probably the correct one: If your mate commits adultery, you may divorce him or her and remarry someone else. While most people agree that divorce is permissible under these circumstances, some question the implied right to remarry. But Jesus is clearly addressing the issue of one who divorces and "marries another," saying that it is wrong to do so *except* in the case of unfaithfulness. Therefore, in the case of immorality or unfaithfulness, it's permissible if someone divorces and marries another person.

Additionally, in Jesus's day adultery was punishable by death. That means the innocent mate in an adulterous marriage often became a widow. And it is clearly understood in the Bible that a widow is free to remarry (see Romans 7:2 and 1 Corinthians 7:39). The fact that we live in a more lenient culture in which adulterers are not executed does not negate the innocent party's right to remarry, though he or she is certainly under no obligation to do so.

The second situation in which divorce and remarriage are allowable is *desertion*. In 1 Corinthians 7, Paul reaffirmed Jesus's teaching that marriage is a lifetime commitment:

> To the married I give instructions, not I, but the Lord, that the wife should not leave her husband. (1 Corinthians 7:10)

However, with the rapid spread of Christianity, some believers were finding themselves in spiritually mixed marriages. One partner might come to faith in Christ while the other remained unconverted. Was the Christian to remain married or should she divorce her unsaved mate and marry a believer? Paul answered this question by posing three different scenarios:

1. What if a Christian finds herself in an unbearable marriage with an unbeliever or perhaps a believer who acts like an unbeliever? Perhaps the Christian is constantly berated for her faith or is subjected to verbal and/or physical abuse. The whole environment of the home is poisoned by anger and fear. Paul said that in this case a Christian may divorce her mate but must remain single or be reconciled to her spouse. Remarriage to another person is not an option if there has been no adultery: "(If she does leave, she must remain unmarried, or else be reconciled to her husband), and the husband should not divorce his wife" (1 Corinthians 7:11).

2. What if a Christian desires to leave his unbelieving wife and marry a believer? Doesn't God want believers only to marry other Christians? Aren't divorce and remarriage in this situation an obligation? No! Paul's "unequally yoked" principle only applies to those who are unmarried and searching for a mate. It has nothing to do with replacing a mate! First

Corinthians 7:12 says, "If any brother has a wife who is an unbeliever, and she consents to live with him, he must not divorce her."

3. What if a Christian is deserted by his non-Christian mate? One of the most helpful truths I have discovered in life is that I cannot control other people's choices. No matter how much emotional energy I expend in attempting to persuade or prevent someone else from taking certain actions, I ultimately have no power over, or responsibility for, another person's choices. The apostle Paul applied this truth to marriage: "If the unbelieving one leaves, let him leave; the brother or the sister is not under bondage in such cases, but God has called us to peace" (1 Corinthians 7:15). If your mate chooses to leave you, you cannot stop him or her. In that situation you are "free to be married"—a phrase Paul used in verse 39 to refer to the right of widows to remarry.

Through the years, people have asked me, "But doesn't this passage apply only to a non-Christian mate who leaves? What if my spouse is a Christian and deserts me? Am I free to remarry?" My response is that we can never know with absolute certainty the spiritual condition of our mate. However, if our spouse abandons the marriage, he or she is certainly *acting* like a non-Christian. As Jesus said, "You will know them by their fruits" (Matthew 7:16). Thus, I believe this allowance for divorce and remarriage also applies to someone who has been abandoned by a so-called Christian mate.

To summarize, both Jesus and Paul taught that God intends marriage to be a lifetime commitment. Nevertheless, they allowed for the possibility of divorce and remarriage in two—and only two—situations: adultery and desertion. In every other situation, we should remain married. If our marriage is intolerable and we choose to divorce our mate, we must either remain single or be reunited with our mate.

Although grace does allow for the possibility of divorce and remarriage, we need to remember God's original purpose for marriage…

Good Grace Emphasizes God's Desire for Permanence in Marriage

Let's return to God's original blueprint for marriage that Moses first recorded in Genesis 2 and Jesus later reaffirmed in Matthew 19:

> Therefore shall a man leave his father and his mother, and shall
> cleave unto his wife: and they shall be one flesh. (Genesis 2:24, KJV)

The Hebrew word *cleave* refers to an unbreakable bond that exists between two people who come together in marriage. The husband and wife are joined together emotionally and spiritually as well as physically. Significantly, this word is used elsewhere in the Old Testament to describe the bond that exists between God and His people:

> You shall fear the LORD your God; you shall serve Him and cling
> ["cleave"] to Him, and you shall swear by His name. (Deuteronomy
> 10:20)

> Be very careful to observe the commandment and the law which
> Moses the servant of the LORD commanded you, to love the LORD
> your God and walk in all His ways and keep His commandments
> and hold fast ["cleave"] to Him and serve Him with all your heart
> and with all your soul. (Joshua 22:5)

God doesn't say to us, "I want to have a relationship with you forever, unless, of course, either you or I fall 'out of love' with each other and find ourselves attracted to someone else. In that case, we are free to follow our hearts." Such an idea is absurd! Our relationship with God is forever.

God uses the same word to describe the commitment we are to exhibit toward our mate. We have been joined together physically, emotionally, and spiritually with our spouse to the extent that we are no longer two persons but one:

> They are no longer two, but one flesh. What therefore God has
> joined together, let no man separate. (Matthew 19:6)

The other day I picked up a packet of photos we had left at the drugstore for developing. As I was looking through the pictures, I noticed that a gluelike substance from the packet had found its way inside, causing two of the photographs to stick together. In spite of my efforts to "uncleave" the photographs, I ended up destroying both pictures.

God doesn't hate divorced people, but He does hate divorce because of what it does to the individuals in a marriage. Here are some of the natural results of divorce:

- "Divorce dramatically increases the likelihood of early death from strokes, hypertension, respiratory cancer, and intestinal cancer. Astonishingly, being divorced and a nonsmoker is only slightly less dangerous than smoking a pack or more a day and staying married!

- "Divorce also disrupts mental health, especially for men. The suicide rate for white males goes up by a factor of four with divorce, and they have ten times the probability of needing psychiatric care.

- "Divorce takes a devastating toll on children. Proportionately twice as many criminals come from single-parent homes. Indeed, family structure proves more effective than economic status in predicting a life in crime. Children from broken homes are more likely to do poorly in school, abuse drugs, and attempt suicide."[1]

Divorce not only destroys the marriage relationship, but it also destroys the two individuals who have been joined together in that union. You cannot tear apart a marriage without also tearing apart the individuals who make up a marriage.

Recently a friend confided to me that her husband had been involved in a long-term sexual affair with another woman. When confronted with his adultery, the husband had promised to break off the relationship. However, my friend discovered that her husband and his mistress were continuing to meet when he was out of town on business. "Give me another chance," he pleaded when his wife presented him with the indisputable evidence of the continuing affair.

"I'm not sure how much longer I can take this. Should I divorce him?" she asked. She certainly had biblical grounds for divorce. Her fatigue from more than a year of riding the emotional roller coaster of hope and despair was understandable. The prospect of a new husband who was committed to loving her exclusively was also appealing.

But her husband had asked for grace, and after a long and probing conversation to collect all the facts, that is what I counseled her to offer him—*if at all possible*. Not just for his benefit, but for hers as well. I reminded her of something a divorce attorney said years ago: "There are two processes that should never be entered into prematurely: embalming and divorce." Why? Because both processes involve death.

Good grace acknowledges that in some circumstances divorce is unavoidable.

Good grace never condemns those who divorce and remarry for biblical reasons.

But a proper understanding of grace will always treat divorce as a last resort in a troubled marriage. It will encourage the innocent spouse to be a dispenser of grace, not justice, when sincerely asked.

After all, isn't that what we desire from God?

CHAPTER NINE

Good Grace Churches

A few days ago one of our Bible-study leaders called to inform me that a member of her small group had just returned home from the hospital after undergoing serious cancer surgery. "Janis would like to talk with you about her funeral service. Would you go by and see her?"

The next day I went to visit Janis, a middle-aged wife and mother who had been in seemingly good health until she had been diagnosed with ovarian cancer ten months earlier. Her husband, Jack, answered the door and ushered me into their living room where Janis lay in a hospital bed, surrounded by her sister, daughter, and husband of thirty-five years. After a few awkward pleasantries, Janis was ready to get down to business. She wanted me to assure her that her memorial service would be a celebration of her homegoing. She had already selected the songs she wanted sung and the Scripture passages she wanted read. Pointing to her burgundy Bible, she said, "Tell the people that I believe every word in that Book!"

As we stood around her bed, we recited a passage from John 14 together and then sang "Amazing Grace" as tears streamed down our faces. We would sing this song again a few days later at her funeral.

Standing beside me on the front steps, her husband said, "Pastor, this is so hard, but I thank God for our church. Our Bible-study group has been here every day bringing food, and they even mowed our lawn. I don't know how people make it through an experience like this without a church."

Yes, I know about the flaws and foibles of the local church. Trust me, any pastor knows *all* about them. Many church members can identify with Mark Buchanan's observation:

> I assume you're like me: I can get itchy-skinned and scratchy-throated after an hour or so of church. I can get distracted and cranky when it goes too long. My feet ache, my backside numbs, my eyes glaze, my mind fogs, my belly growls, I find myself fighting back yawns.... And I'm the pastor.[1]

Mediocre sermons, dictatorial leaders, hypocritical members, and judgmental attitudes are just some of the problems that occur whenever imperfect people are joined together in a spiritual community. As my friend Howard Hendricks says, "The church is a lot like Noah's ark. If it weren't for the storm on the outside, we couldn't stand the stench on the inside."

Yes, occasional odors emanate from within the walls of a church, but a relentless storm also rages on the outside, making us grateful that God has provided a spiritual shelter for us.

For a moment consider some the benefits that may have come into your life through a local body of believers who joined together to fulfill the Great Commission. Perhaps you are thinking about...

- someone who took a personal interest in your spiritual condition and shared the gospel of Christ with you.
- a pastor or Bible-study leader who opened your eyes to the value of studying God's Word.
- a small group of believers who committed to pray with you about a difficult circumstance in your life.
- a support group that surrounded you when you lost a loved one.

- the refreshment that comes each Sunday when you are able to leave behind a week's worth of problems and engage in exhilarating worship.

Can you imagine what life would be like without your church? Most of us would not want to even consider such a possibility. We are grateful (most of the time) for the spiritual benefits that accrue to us through the church. Yet in spite of the mostly warm feelings we have toward the church, Christians today are increasingly treating the church with disdain.

- They consider membership in a local church optional.
- Their attendance is sporadic.
- Their giving is minimal.
- They view ministry as burdensome.
- They believe that sin is permissible.

If the Founder of our faith, Jesus Christ, loved the church so much that He "gave Himself up for her" (Ephesians 5:25), why don't we share the same sacrificial concern for her?

I believe that a distortion of grace is largely responsible for the apathy many Christians demonstrate toward their local congregations. Whenever the importance of membership, the necessity of attendance, the expectations for giving, the responsibility of service, and the need for purity within a local congregation are upheld, the proponents of bad grace yell "Legalism!" causing leaders to back off from upholding such biblical standards.

The result? Many Christians question whether membership in a church is even necessary. Weekly attendance continues to fall, financial support for churches is at an all-time low, volunteer positions are difficult to fill, and unconfronted sin continues to neutralize the church's witness to the world.

If the church is not only to survive—which Jesus promised she would—but thrive, we must rescue her from the hands of bad grace before it is too late. It is time to reaffirm the responsibilities we have toward the church that Jesus Christ founded and for which He poured out His life. In the next two chapters, we are going to contrast bad grace and good grace in four specific areas related to the church.

Regarding Membership

Bad grace says, "I don't need to join a church."

Good grace says, "God has provided a church for me to join."

Every week numerous visitors attend our services. While some are non-Christians, the majority of our guests are believers who have recently moved into our area and are searching for a church home. But increasingly, our staff is hearing this response from guests: "We will continue to attend, but we don't intend to become members. We're just not 'joiners.'" Other pastors I talk with are hearing the same responses. Indeed, George Gallup once said that most believers today think they can be "good" Christians without joining a local church.

Do we have to join a church to be a good Christian? I could answer that question by pointing out the New Testament passages that indicate membership in the first-century church was the norm for believers. The early church had structure, requirements, and membership rolls. They even counted their new members (a tradition my fellow Baptists are more than happy to continue).

But the real question is not "Do I *have* to join a church to be a good Christian?" but "Do I *need* to join a church to be a good Christian?" And the answer is yes. God did not create the church because He was looking for a way to waste our time, sap our finances, or frustrate our joy. God designed the church just as much for our benefit as for His. The church is God's gift to us.

Although this list is not exhaustive, allow me to highlight some of the reasons we need the church.

1. The church provides the instruction we need for our spiritual growth. A primary function of the early church was instruction in "the apostles' teaching" (Acts 2:42). Before Christians possessed the written Word of God, they obviously needed to gather together frequently to hear Jesus's handpicked teachers—also known as the apostles. Today, of course, "the apostles' teaching" has been deposited in the Bible and is available to everyone. However, our ability to read the Word of God for ourselves does not negate our need to be taught by godly and gifted teachers. God established the office of pastor for the primary purpose of teaching other Christians:

> He gave some as...pastors and *teachers,* for the equipping of the saints for the work of service, to the building up of the body of Christ. (Ephesians 4:11-12)

> An overseer [pastor], then, must be above reproach,...*able to teach.* (1 Timothy 3:2)

> The elders who rule well are to be considered worthy of double honor, especially those who work hard at *preaching and teaching.* (1 Timothy 5:17)

> Pay close attention to yourself and to your *teaching;* persevere in these things, for as you do this you will ensure salvation both for yourself and for those who hear you. (1 Timothy 4:16)

While the Holy Spirit is our *primary* Teacher of spiritual truth, He is not our *only* Teacher. The pastor, as well as other gifted teachers within a congregation, is often the mouthpiece through whom the Holy Spirit instructs us.

2. The church provides encouragement when we become discouraged. One of Satan's favorite tactics for destroying Christians is to isolate them from other believers and then attack them with temptation, depression, illness, financial loss, or the death of a loved one. Even though a Christian is indwelt by the Holy Spirit of God, a solitary Christian is usually no match for the unending attacks of the Evil One. That realization led Solomon to make this observation:

> Two are better than one because they have a good return for their labor. For if either of them falls, the one will lift up his companion. But woe to the one who falls when there is not another to lift him up. (Ecclesiastes 4:9-10)

A Christian never needs to face Satan's attacks alone. God has given us a simple strategy for spiritual success: Bind yourself together with other Christians who can help you resist the Enemy.

> If one can overpower him who is alone, two can resist him. A cord of three strands is not quickly torn apart. (Ecclesiastes 4:12)

God understands that there is strength in numbers! When we are under unrelenting attack, we need other Christians who will pray for us when we become discouraged, remind us of the spiritual battle in which we are engaged, and love us and lift us back up when we fail. That is what the church is all about.

3. The church provides accountability when we wander. A popular cable talk-show host wrote a best-selling book several years ago titled *Who's Looking Out for You?* The inference was that he was serving as our advocate by holding public officials accountable for their actions.

But as well intentioned as the author might be, he is really incapable of watching out for me personally. Seated in his television studio in New York, he wouldn't know if I'm cheating on my wife, refusing to let go of bitterness, or drifting in my relationship with God. Sadly, he doesn't even know my name!

Fortunately, God has provided a guardian for my spiritual well-being that is much closer to home. It's called the church. In Hebrews 13:17 the writer explains why we are to obey the spiritual leaders in our local church. But in doing so, he also describes one significant benefit of being a member of a congregation: "Obey your leaders and submit to them, *for they keep watch over your souls* as those who will give an account."

Ideally, godly leaders and concerned members link together to form a spiritual fence to keep us from wandering from God's pasture into Satan's field. This is such an important function of the church that we will explore it further in the next chapter.

4. The church provides a more powerful witness to the world than one beliver can. Our culture's emphasis on individualism spills over into our attitude toward the church. We tend to focus on the needs and potential of the individual believer rather than of the group as a whole. We talk about discovering *your* spiritual gift, finding *your* purpose in life, developing *your* relationship with God. But the Bible describes the church not as a collection of individuals but as a body. "Now you are Christ's body, and individually members of it" (1 Corinthians 12:27). Our Western mind-set causes us to bypass the word *body* and zero in on the word *individually*. We fail to understand the unity of the body of Christ that Paul describes and, instead, only emphasize the diversity within the body.

"Just as the human body has many parts, so does the body of Christ. We are not all eyes, or ears or feet. Imagine if our body were one giant eyeball or one giant ear! God created us for different roles in the church. We need to discover our individual gifts and use them," Paul explained. (See 1 Corinthians 12:14-22.) While diversity among Christians is *a* truth in this passage, it is not the *only* truth.

Just as important as diversity in the body of Christ is unity:

Even as the body is one and yet has many members, and all the members of the body, though they are many, are one body, so also is Christ.… And the eye cannot say to the hand, "I have no need of you"; or again the head to the feet, "I have no need of you." (1 Corinthians 12:12,21)

An eyeball, a hand, or a foot is useless by itself. But when they are joined together in a body, the sum becomes greater than the individual parts.

The same principle applies in the church. Christians joined together in a church have a greater impact on the world as well as on one another than they have individually. A spiritual synergy occurs when Christians band together. A community is much more likely to feel the impact of a group of Christians who are gathered and organized to fulfill the Great Commission than the same number of Christians who are operating as independent agents.

Our church has just completed building a new worship center. A few months ago I sat in on a committee meeting with the architects and was surprised to learn of an additional expense that we had not anticipated but was required for new structures: emergency lighting. You have probably noticed those small lights on the edge of the aisles in movie theaters. (Since this is a book on grace, it's all right to admit that you go to the movies.) Even when the theater is dark, these lights remain on to help people find their way when everything around them is pitch black.

When I discovered the cost of these lights, I was astounded. "Couldn't we get by with just a few lights?" I asked hopefully. I could have argued that a single light on row 56 should be sufficient. "After all, who can really measure the impact of one solitary light?" I might have pleaded. I could have told all kinds of heartrending stories about how a single light had made a difference throughout history. But the city building codes would not accommodate my cheapness. If one light is beneficial, two hundred lights are even more helpful to point people to safety in a dark room.

Although every Christian's individual witness is valuable, we should never underestimate the importance of our collective influence through the church. That is why Paul referred to believers as those who "appear as *lights* in the world" (Philippians 2:15). After all, to paraphrase Solomon, two bulbs are better than one, and a group of three cannot easily be ignored.

I love the way one writer describes the benefits of the local church:

> There is nothing like the local church when it's working right. Its beauty is indescribable. Its power is breathtaking. Its potential is unlimited. It comforts the grieving and heals the broken in the context of community. It builds bridges to seekers and offers truth to the confused. It provides resources for those in need and opens its arms to the forgotten, the downtrodden, the disillusioned. It breaks the chains of addictions, frees the oppressed, and offers belonging to the marginalized of this world. Whatever the capacity for human suffering, the church has a greater capacity for healing and wholeness.[2]

When you put it like that, membership in a church is not only a duty; it is an indescribable privilege!

REGARDING ATTENDANCE

Bad grace says, "I can miss church as often as I want."

Good grace says, "I should attend as frequently as I can."

Do you remember "Pastor Jerry" from the first chapter? Yes, I'll admit it; I'm the one who drove past those tennis courts that Easter Sunday morning and saw them filled with student and parents, many of whom no doubt were Christians who seemed to feel completely at ease with choosing tennis over church. I didn't have the same apoplectic reaction as my fictional counterpart, but that experience crystallized in my mind the need for this book.

Why is it that church attendance in general is declining? The pollsters will point to uninvolvement of the laity, poor preaching, distrust of leaders, and failure to meet the felt needs of the congregation as reasons for the decline—and that's just in *my* church.

While these are all convenient excuses for skipping Sunday services, I believe a misunderstanding of grace has fostered the capricious attitude many Christians have toward church attendance. Grace, we are led to believe, exempts us from any standard regarding participation in church. Recently a Bible-study leader in our church was absent from his class as much as he was present. When a staff member gently reminded him of his need to be in class more often, he bristled, "That's legalism. I'm under grace."

But those who use grace as an excuse for excessive absences fail to understand two simple reasons we need to be in church every Sunday we possibly can be:

1. Your presence makes a difference to others. In our narcissistic world we confine our thinking about church to the "What's in it for me?" syndrome. We rarely consider how our absence affects others. But the writer of Hebrews explained the relationship between our attendance and the spiritual health of fellow believers:

> Let us consider how to stimulate one another to love and good
> deeds, not forsaking our own assembling together, as is the habit
> of some, but encouraging one another. (10:24-25)

No Christian is an island. We are to look beyond ourselves and remember our responsibility to build up (the meaning of the word *edify*) other

Christians. One practical way we do that is by joining together with other Christians each week for worship and instruction.

How does my presence encourage other Christians? Have you ever walked into a church that was half-empty? I don't believe pastors are the only ones who are discouraged by sparse attendance. When you see more empty pews than people, you naturally wonder, *What's wrong with this place?* and may question why you are wasting your time there if so many other people have opted out.

Have you ever attended a Bible-study class when the teacher was gone and you had to endure teaching from someone who was obviously unqualified? Did the experience make you want to come back for another helping of mediocrity?

Have you ever come to church in need of encouragement but left empty-hearted because no one spoke to you?

Your presence in a local congregation can make a difference! When you are not in church, it means that...

- One less voice is singing God's praises.
- One less prayer is being offered before the throne of grace.
- One less person is available to meet the needs of hurting Christians.
- One less spiritual gift is being exercised to help perfect the body of Christ.
- One less believer is present to hear vital instruction from God's Word that will help that person impact the world for Christ.

The impact we have on the lives of other Christians is one reason we need to regularly attend our church. But this is not the only reason.

2. Your presence makes a difference in your own life. If you grew up in a home with caring parents, they probably had some well-established rules. They insisted on a curfew to ensure you got enough rest. They offered balanced meals for your physical development. If you were sick, they took you to the doctor.

But then came the day you left your parents' home and were suddenly on your own. Today does anyone make sure you get enough sleep, insist that you eat properly, or encourage you to exercise? Probably not. But if you are wise, you will do those things anyway for your own benefit.

When it comes to involvement in the local church, proponents of bad grace remind me of college freshmen who are out from under their parents' thumb for the first time. They are so intoxicated with their newfound freedom that they often make unwise choices about diet, rest, exercise, and other health-related issues. Hopefully, they wake up one day and realize the wisdom of their parents' instructions.

Similarly, bad gracers are so fixated on their freedom that they neglect their responsibilities, not only toward others, but toward themselves.

As we have already seen in Galatians 4, Paul declared that we are no longer children being held under bondage by the Old Testament law. Christ has freed us from all those regulations about diet, dress, and religious ritual.

But we have been so quick to throw out the Old Testament law regarding the strict observance of the Sabbath that we have also discarded an important principle that transcends the two Testaments: We still need one day a week when we refuse to work and, instead, focus on our relationship with God in a congregation of other believers. Even though the day has changed from Saturday to Sunday and the location has switched from the temple or synagogue to the church, regular worship is still important for our emotional and spiritual health.

—

In the next chapter we'll discover how good grace affects two additional responsibilities—and privileges—every Christian has in the local church.

CHAPTER TEN

Good Grace Giving

R on had been out of work for more than six months when he came to visit with me.

"Pastor, I have some good news. I just landed a job. But I have a question for you. During the time I was unemployed, we depleted our savings and incurred quite a bit of credit-card debt. We have no emergency fund or money set aside for our daughter's college tuition. Sara is supposed to enroll in the university this fall. Here's my question. Should we continue to give 10 percent of our income to the church, or should we first pay off our credit-card bills and replenish our daughter's college fund?"

How would you answer Ron's question?

How does good grace impact our attitude about investing both our financial resources and time in God's kingdom through the local church? The contrast between good grace and bad grace concerning our stewardship of money and time is a stark one:

Bad grace says, "I can give as little as I want."

Good grace says, "I should give as much as I can."

A Delicate Issue

Having just completed a twenty-one-million-dollar campaign for our church's new worship center, I can assure you that no subject evokes more controversy and results in more misunderstanding than giving. As a pastor I have discovered an important anatomical insight: The most sensitive part of the human body is the pocketbook! Furthermore, even if it is agreed that we should invest our financial resources in God's work, there is little consensus about how much we should give.

Some Christians take a very rigid view regarding tithing and believe we should give 10 percent of our gross income to God's work. These folks would tell Ron that the first 10 percent of his paycheck goes to the church, regardless of creditors or family obligations. They would quote Malachi 3:8-9, which equates a failure to tithe with robbing God. To the charge that the tithe is part of the Old Testament law that no longer applies to Christians today, they would point out that Abraham tithed four hundred years before the Old Testament law was communicated to Moses (see Genesis 14:20). Furthermore, Jesus commended the Pharisees for tithing, even though He condemned them for ignoring other parts of the Law (see Matthew 23:23). Thus, the tithe continues to be God's standard for giving today. Period.

However, others question whether the 10 percent rule applies today. They argue that under the Old Testament law, Jews actually gave three tithes—10 percent each year to support the Levites, an additional 10 percent annually for special celebrations, and another 10 percent every third year for special needs among the people—which amounted to 23.3 percent of their income given to God each year. So not even the Israelites practiced the 10 percent rule.

Additionally, they say, except for Jesus's acknowledgment that the Pharisees tithed, there is no explicit command in the New Testament for Christians to give 10 percent of their income to the church. Instead, Paul instructed each member of the Corinthian congregation to give "as God [has] prospered him" (1 Corinthians 16:2, KJV).

Most Christians, by practice if not by profession, believe that the tithe is no longer the standard for giving today. They practice what is often referred to as "grace giving." Unfortunately, grace giving for most Christians means giving as little as possible without being overwhelmed by guilt. Apparently most grace givers have a very high threshold for guilt! According to a recent study, giving to churches as a percentage of income has been steadily declining since 1961 and today is less than 3 percent. Amazingly, giving to churches today as a percent of income is less than it was in 1933 during the Great Depression![1]

A true understanding about the relationship between grace and giving will produce much different results. While I will admit that there is no one-percentage-fits-all standard for giving, there are three important principles about stewardship that, if applied, will result in more, not less, financial investment in God's kingdom.

1. "Everything I have belongs to God." One of the downsides of insisting on 10 percent as the standard for giving is the implication that the other 90 percent of our money belongs to us. But, as God reminded Job, "Everything under heaven belongs to me" (Job 41:11, NIV). I want you to stop here for a moment and repeat this phrase out loud: "Everything I have belongs to God."

Try saying it again. "*Everything* I have belongs to God."

Now, one more time with all the enthusiasm you can muster. "Everything I have belongs to God!"

As Randy Alcorn observes in his wonderful book *The Treasure Principle,* we tend to act like owners rather than managers. Most of our difficulty in giving to God's work stems from our failure to understand that everything we have is simply on loan to us from God. Alcorn explains the implications of being managers rather than owners of the financial resources we enjoy:

> Our name is on God's account. We have unrestricted access to it, a privilege that is subject to abuse. As His money managers, God trusts us to set our own salaries. We draw needed funds from His wealth to pay our living expenses. One of our central spiritual decisions is determining what is a reasonable amount to live on. Whatever that amount is—and it will legitimately vary from person to person—we shouldn't hoard or spend the excess. After all, it's His, not ours. And He has something to say about where to put it.[2]

The realization that we are managers of God's money leads to a second principle.

2. We should seek the highest rate of return with God's money. Recently I hired a financial advisor to take care of my assets, not because I am so wealthy, but because I believe there are better ways to invest my time than poring over mutual-fund charts. My advisor's fee is based on a percentage of my assets. The more he earns for me, the more he earns for himself. Periodically we meet to review his performance. If we have had an "up" year, I commend him. If we've lost money, I frown and encourage him to do better. But his real incentive for superior performance is the compensation he receives.

In Matthew 25 Jesus told a parable about a man who was leaving on a journey and entrusted his possessions to three of his employees. He divided his assets according to the financial acumen of the individual employees. One received five talents (about four hundred pounds of silver), another received half that amount, and the third employee received only one talent.

After a long period of time, the master returned and asked for an accounting of how his employees had handled the money. Two of the employees had doubled the amount entrusted to them. But the third employee played it safe and buried his talent. The master commended the two men who had doubled their investments, but he condemned the employee who had earned zilch.

The master then did something most would consider profoundly unjust. He took the one talent that the employee had carefully guarded and gave it to the employee who had ten talents. "How unfair!" we protest. "The wealthy employee doesn't need any more talents; he already has ten. He should be forced to give some of his talents to that poor guy who has only one. The master needs to distribute his wealth more evenly!"

But Jesus explained that in God's economy, those who make good investments on His behalf will be given more, and those who fail to increase the resources on loan to them will have them taken away.

This parable reminds us that one day we will give an account to the Master for how we have used the time, talents, and treasure He has entrusted to us. Our future rewards in heaven will be determined, in part, by the way we have managed the money God has loaned us. That is why Jesus offered this word of financial advice to all of us:

Do not store up for yourselves treasures on earth, where moth and
rust destroy, and where thieves break in and steal. But store up for
yourselves treasures in heaven, where neither moth nor rust destroys,
and where thieves do not break in and steal; for where your treasure
is, there will your heart will be also. (Matthew 6:19-21)

Obviously, some of our "treasure" here on earth should be spent on the necessities of everyday life, such as food, shelter, clothing, or even occasional splurges that remove some of the tedium of everyday life. But Jesus reminds us that everything we purchase here on earth is subject to destruction—or at least severe depreciation. Everyone who has ever lost money in the stock market or held a garage sale and watched items bought only a few years ago sold for pennies on the dollar understands that truth.

However, money invested in God's work is safe from destruction and depreciation. Furthermore, those assets will reap dividends for us throughout eternity!

For example, suppose you were walking down the streets of Bethlehem two thousand years ago, and you heard that the Messiah had been born. You thought to yourself, *I believe this guy may be the one!* and you decided to invest in his life and ministry. Let's suppose you invested one dollar and that dollar earned 6 percent compounded interest every year. Do you know how much that one dollar you invested instead of buying a bagel and a cup of coffee would be worth today? How about $720 quadrillion![3]

"Yeah," you wonder cynically, "but who is going to live two thousand years to see that kind of return?" You are. In fact, you are going to live for all eternity. That means every dollar you invest today in God's kingdom enterprise is going to multiply at a much greater rate than 6 percent and will yield dividends for all eternity!

That realization changes our attitude toward giving from "How little can I give and still look respectable?" to "How much money can I scrape together and pour into this no-lose investment?" Nevertheless, most of us need some rule of thumb for determining a reasonable amount to invest in God's work while taking care of the other obligations we have as residents of this planet. That leads to a third principle.

3. The tithe should be the starting place for most Christians. As you look through the Bible, the tithe seems to be a standard for giving that was initiated by Abraham four hundred years before God gave the Law to Israel. As we saw, the Jews, who lived mostly in poverty, gave substantially more than 10 percent of their income to support God's work each year. Why would we who live in the wealthiest country in the history of world ever do less? Ultimately, the decision of how much to give is a heart issue, not a pocketbook issue.

I remember hearing a sermon by Dr. Bob Russell in which he told of a group from his church returning from a mission trip to Romania. The group members were especially impressed by the Romanian Christians' attitude toward giving. These believers were convinced that they should be giving a tithe to the church, but the government allowed citizens to contribute only 2.5 percent of their income to charitable organizations. So they began searching for ways to circumvent or change the law so that they could give the full 10 percent to God's church. Pastor Russell said to his congregation, "The Romanian Christians have less, and they're looking for a way to give 10 percent, and we're free to give as we please. In fact, we get a tax break for doing so, and we're looking for loopholes in the Scripture to avoid doing it. What an indictment!"

True grace giving will always lead us to give as much, not as little, as we possibly can.

Regarding Service

Bad grace says, "I don't have to do anything in the church."

Good grace says, "God has given me the privilege of serving somewhere in the church."

Tom and Renee Davis were tired. For fifteen years they had been members of Elmwood Baptist Church (the church where Pastor Jerry threw his Easter-morning tantrum). For the past ten years they have served in the nursery on Sunday morning instead of attending a Bible-study class with their own age group. Renee is a member of the women's ministries council, and Tom serves as vice-chairman of the deacons, head usher, and chairman of the finance committee.

Although Tom and Renee are supportive of Pastor Jerry, Tom has grown tired of the battles he has to fight in the finance committee with disgruntled members who are less than enthused over their pastor's vision for the church.

"Honey, I think we need a change," Tom told his wife after another grueling committee meeting.

The next Sunday the Davises sneaked over to Living Waters Fellowship where Pastor Chip pressed the right button for them.

"Are you tired of the treadmill of endless activities? Have you spent so much time doing things for God that you've forgotten that all He really wants is a relationship with you? Most churches fail to understand that God is much more interested in our character than in our service. He is more concerned with who we are than in what we do. That is why at our church you will never be harassed into filling some slot. We believe our church exists for you and not vice versa."

Tom and Renee felt as if they had stumbled upon an oasis. Pastor Chip's words were just what their parched souls needed to hear. They desperately needed a sabbatical from ministry, so the following week they informed Pastor Jerry that they were resigning all their positions so that they could take some time off. But, they assured him, they would probably be back. Three years later Tom and Renee were still at Living Waters Fellowship being "nourished back to spiritual health," as Renee explained to her friends—and completely free of any responsibilities.

Congregations that promote bad grace portray involvement in ministry—especially ministries within the local church—as optional rather than essential. If, *after* you have fulfilled your work responsibilities, indulged yourself in your hobbies, and spent all the quality time with your family you can possibly stand, you still have some hours left in the week, then you *might* want to assume a place of responsibility in the church. Otherwise, don't feel obligated.

But good grace understands that ministry in a local body of believers is a privilege as well as a responsibility. Service in a church is not an attempt to earn God's grace; it is the *result* of receiving God's grace. In an act of inexplicable compassion, God not only declares those of us who had been His enemies to be His friends, but He also invites us to join with Him in building His kingdom.

Can you imagine a prisoner of war of a defeated army who is facing execution being summoned before the commanding general and told, "You have been pardoned of your crimes. And not only that, I have decided to make you a captain in our army with all the rights and privileges that position warrants"? That is exactly what God has done for us! Not only have we who were facing eternal death have been pardoned, but we have been selected to work with God in the advancement of His empire.

"Robert, aren't you stretching just a little here? Is there really a relationship between grace and service in the church?" Glad you asked! Notice how Paul related grace to service in Romans 12:

Since we have gifts that differ according to the *grace* given to us,
each of us is to exercise them accordingly: if prophecy, according
to the proportion of his faith; if service, in his serving; or he who
teaches, in his teaching; or he who exhorts, in his exhortation; he
who gives, with liberality; he who leads, with diligence; he who
shows mercy, with cheerfulness. (verses 6-8)

Obviously, I could devote an entire book or two to the subject of spiritual gifts, but allow me to point out three simple truths that emerge from these verses:

1. Every Christian has been given a unique spiritual gift. Of course, the ultimate Gift we possess is the Holy Spirit of God, but when He comes

into our lives, He brings with Him a unique gift to use in God's service. Like you, I've seen many definitions of *spiritual gift*, but this is my favorite (and it happens to be my own): A spiritual gift is the unique passion and power God gives you to further His kingdom.

A spiritual gift is a special desire or passion that burns within you. Some people love to teach the Bible. Others think that meeting the practical needs of others is the best way to demonstrate the love of Christ. Still others believe that showing genuine concern to those who are hurting is their niche. Discover your passion and start using it, Paul says!

According to one writer, "Our world is incomplete until each one of us discovers what moves us—our passion. No other person can hear our calling. We must listen and act on it for ourselves."[4]

For our discussion, allow me to tweak that statement just a bit: The kingdom of God is incomplete until each one of us discovers what moves us—our passion. No other person can hear our calling. We must listen and act on it for others.

Not only is a spiritual gift a passion, it is also a power that God grants us. Noted Greek lexicographer Henry Thayer defines a spiritual gift as an "extraordinary power, distinguishing certain Christians and enabling them to serve the church of Christ, the reception of which is due to the power of divine grace operating in their souls by the Holy Spirit."

When God gives you a special calling, He also gives you the power to fulfill that calling. If your gift is teaching the Bible, then not only will you enjoy teaching, you will also be empowered to teach. If your gift is mercy, God will enable you to discern the needs of others. If your gift is giving, God will grant you an unusual ability to multiply your assets so they can be used for His work.

2. Our spiritual gifts are to be used in the local church. The context of Paul's discussion about spiritual gifts is his comparison between our physical body and the body of Christ:

We, who are many, are one body in Christ, and individually members one of another. (Romans 12:5)

Just as our eyes, ears, and feet function as parts of our body, not independently or as parts of someone else's body, we are to exercise our gifts as part of the church, which is the body of Christ. The word *church* (which means "called out ones") is occasionally used in the New Testament to refer to all Christians everywhere and would not only include Christians here on earth but those already in heaven.

But of the more than one hundred references to the church in the New Testament, more than ninety of them refer to a local church, which my friend Charles Ryrie defines as a "group of baptized believers who have organized themselves for the purpose of doing God's will."

The local church is God's creation, not man's. While other Christian organizations may have legitimate and vital ministries, they are no substitute for the local church. Only the church has God's promise of enduring until the Lord returns. That is why our gifts should be used, as Thayer says, "to serve the church of Christ."

In our church we have a saying: No one can do everything, but everyone can do something. Once every six months we distribute a list of the various opportunities for service in the church and encourage our members to find at least one ministry in which they can exercise their gift, whether as an usher, a bus driver, a Bible-study leader, or a television camera technician.

Remember, God gave you a gift to use. "Since we have gifts...each of us is to exercise them" (Romans 12:6). Where are you exercising your gift?

3. Fulfillment comes from using our spiritual gifts. I don't believe it is any accident that the same word Paul uses for "gift" in Romans 12 *(charismaton)* is not only linked to the word for "grace" *(charis)* but also has as its root word *joy (char).* Exercising our God-given spiritual gifts in the church brings incredible joy in our lives when we understand how God is using us in an enterprise that is so much bigger than we are.

At the root of apathy—the tedium of everyday life that makes it increasingly difficult for so many to get out of bed every morning and pursue life with any enthusiasm—is a lack of purpose. John Eldredge writes,

> For years all my daily energy was spent trying to beat the trials in my life and arrange for a little pleasure. My weeks were wasted away either striving or indulging. I was a mercenary. A mercenary fights for pay, for his own benefit; his life is devoted to himself. "The quality of a true warrior," says Bly, "is that he is in service to a purpose greater than himself; that is, to a transcendent cause."[5]

The "transcendent cause" to which you and I have been called is the building of the kingdom of God. And He has entrusted to us a unique passion and power to accomplish that highest of all callings.

But can using my gift in a local congregation *really* make an eternal difference?

Consider the ministry of one Sunday-school teacher who taught a group of older teenagers in his local church. The teacher had been concerned about an eighteen-year-old boy in his class who had seemed distracted and disinterested. One day the teacher visited the teenager at the job where he was working. He explained to his student that he had felt impressed to share with him how much Jesus loved him. And right there in the store, the teenager trusted in Christ as his Savior. The teacher's name was Edward Kimball. The teenager's name was Dwight L. Moody.[6]

Since that day in April 1855, millions of people have been impacted by the ministry of D. L. Moody through his evangelistic preaching, and later by the Moody Bible Institute in Chicago, the Moody Radio Network, and Moody Publishers.

But Moody's influence continued through others. The great evangelist once counseled a young man named J. Wilbur Chapman, who later became a Presbyterian minister. Chapman and Moody together impacted the life of Billy Sunday, another gifted evangelist who led more than two-hundred-thousand people to faith in Christ.[7]

In 1924, Billy Sunday conducted an evangelistic crusade in Charlotte, North Carolina, from which the Charlotte Businessman's Club was established. In 1934, this group of Christian businessmen asked an evangelist named Mordecai Ham to speak at a crusade in Charlotte. At one of those services, an eighteen-year-old named Billy Graham came forward to accept Christ as his Savior.[8]

Today hundreds of millions of people around the globe have been impacted by the ministry of Billy Graham. And whether or not they realize it, it can all be traced back to Edward Kimball, a layman serving in a local church who realized that life was about more than earning a living. One person using his or her gift in one church *can* make a world of difference.

Churches that promote good grace do not shirk their responsibility for teaching that membership is necessary, attendance is essential, giving is a responsibility, and service is a privilege.

But there is one other area in church life in which a stark contrast between good grace and bad grace exists. It is subject of such critical importance that it deserves an entire chapter for our consideration.

CHAPTER ELEVEN

Good Grace Confrontation

P astor, there is something I thought you should know," Don said in a subdued voice over a lunch meeting he had called with the new shepherd of Community Hills Church. Those words cause any pastor to tense up, since it's rare that the "something you should know" is anything positive—like the existence of a secret slush fund containing hundreds of thousands of dollars available for his use.

Pastor Dave Ross mentally braced himself for whatever was about to come next.

"One of *your* elders has cheated several of us in the church. Our family alone has lost over twenty thousand dollars we had earmarked for retirement. Some have lost even more."

Don then launched into a detailed description of the failed business venture in which Bill Samuels, the elder in question, had solicited funds from a number of people in the church in order to open a brand-name pizza parlor that catered to children and promised to be an instant success. Months passed, and all that had appeared on the vacant lot was a sign announcing that the restaurant would open "soon." Finally, one of the investors became suspicious, called the headquarters of the restaurant chain, and discovered that they had never heard of Bill Samuels.

When the investors confronted Bill, he was insulted that anyone would question his integrity. He explained that he was simply waiting for an opportune time to purchase the franchise so that he could obtain the best deal possible. Still, after nearly a year, there was no pizza parlor; only excuses.

"Pastor, this is going to split our church unless you do something!" Don insisted.

"What exactly did you have in mind?" Pastor Dave asked.

"Well, doesn't the Bible say something about disciplining church members who sin, and if they don't repent, kick them out of the church?"

Pastor Dave knew the Matthew 18 passage to which Don was alluding. Although he had written an exegetical paper on the passage in seminary and preached several sermons from it in previous churches, he had no experience in actually exercising church discipline.

"Yes, Don, the Bible does say we should confront sinning church members. But it also says that you should go to him in private first. If that doesn't work, then you are to take two or three with you to persuade him."

"We've done that, Pastor, but he hasn't listened. It's time for the church to take action. The entire elder board needs to meet with him. If he doesn't listen, then his membership should be revoked."

Pastor Dave promised to look into the matter but dreaded the prospect of inserting himself into a controversy with so much potential for disruption, especially this early in his tenure.

—=—

Pastor Dave had only been back in his office a few minutes after his lunch with Don when he received a phone call from Bill Beshears, the chairman of the church's education committee.

"Pastor, there's something you need to know."

Oh no. Here we go again, Dave thought.

"I've received several complaints from members of Nancy Wilcox's Bible-study class. They report that she is saying some very critical things about the direction you are leading the church."

"What sort of things?" Dave asked.

"Well, she says that you are trying to turn our church into a seeker-friendly church by diluting the teaching of God's Word from the pulpit in order to attract new members. Apparently others in her class voiced their concerns as well. The member who called me is worried that this could cause a split in our church."

It was true that Pastor Dave had tried to change the worship services at Community Hills to create a more inviting atmosphere for non-Christians. Instead of preaching through books of the Bible like his predecessor, Dave preached topical messages on dealing with marriages, parenting, and friendships. But all his messages had been rooted in Scripture.

How should he deal with Nancy Wilcox, who was not only the most respected Bible teacher in the church but was equally known for being outspoken in her beliefs? If anyone tried to muzzle her, it could make things worse. And didn't she have a right to voice her beliefs? Yet, given the large following she had in the church, her criticism could snowball into an open rebellion against the new pastor's leadership and divide the congregation.

———

Pastor Dave was glad that he had only one appointment scheduled that afternoon. He was ready to go home early after being ambushed by two problems for which there were no easy answers. Dave actually looked forward to meeting with Dianne and Roger, a young couple whom Dave was scheduled to marry in several weeks. Dianne had been a member of Community Hills since she was a little girl and had met Roger during their senior year in college.

As always, Pastor Dave began the premarital counseling session by inquiring about the couple's spiritual lives. Dianne related how she had trusted in Christ as a young girl and just recently had become more serious about her walk with Christ. Roger, however, gave a murky description of his relationship to Christ. When Pastor Dave asked the well-known "What would you say if you were to stand before God and He asked, 'Why should I let you into heaven?'" question, Roger shrugged and said, "I don't know."

For the next thirty minutes, Dave presented the plan of salvation to Roger and led him in a prayer in which Roger asked Jesus Christ to be his Savior. Pastor Dave and Dianne both sensed that Roger's commitment was genuine. Pastor Dave encouraged Roger to be baptized as a sign of his faith in Christ and join the church the following Sunday so that he and Dianne could begin their lives together as members of the same congregation.

As they wrapped up their session, Dave asked Roger for his address so that he could send him some follow-up material. Dave then asked Dianne for her address to send her a book on marriage that he thought they would both enjoy. When she gave the same address as Roger's, Pastor Dave tried to hide his surprise. But neither acting nor poker had been one of Dave's strengths.

"Pastor, we've been living together for the past several months. We know it's wrong, but after all, we are going to be married soon," Dianne confessed.

Pastor Dave was not sure how to respond. He did not want to condemn Roger, a brand-new convert. After all, five minutes ago he was not a Christian, so how could he be expected to know any better? But now that he was a Christian, should Pastor Dave allow him to join the church if he insisted on living with Dianne before their marriage? And if Dave refused membership to Roger, wasn't he also obligated to revoke Dianne's membership if she persisted in this living arrangement? Should he refuse to marry them unless they repented, or should he insist that they move up the date of the marriage?

———

Church discipline. For many of us those two words evoke primarily negative emotions and images. We tend to associate the concept of church discipline with harshness and legalism being administered by dour old men who are more suited to living in the eighteenth century than the twenty-first century. After all, hasn't the "grace awakening" that has swept through our churches today taught us that we shouldn't judge other believers? Shouldn't we be free to believe whatever we choose to believe, say whatever we want to say, and live however we want to live? If we answer only to Jesus Christ, why should we allow anyone else to pass judgment on us? And why should we ever feel compelled to correct another Christian? Don't most of us have enough "planks" to remove from our own eyes before we attempt to remove the "specks" out of other people's eyes?

Bad grace teaches that Christians have no right to judge the behavior of other members in the church. Good grace recognizes that Christians have a responsibility to correct and restore other believers who are living in disobedience. Interestingly, such a responsibility was well understood in other generations. As we will see, numerous New Testament passages exhort us to correct, rebuke, and seek to restore fellow believers who are living in disobedience. Furthermore, if an erring Christian refuses to respond to correction, both Jesus and Paul commanded that he or she be turned out of the church.

For hundreds of years the church took those New Testament instructions at face value. The Belgic Confession (1561), which grew out of the Reformation, stated that the true church is known by three characteristics:

"(a) the preaching of pure doctrine, (b) the administration of the sacraments, and (c) the exercise of church discipline."[1]

During the time of Cotton Mather, Puritans compiled a broad list of sins that warranted official church action against a member, including "swearing, cursing, sabbath-breaking, drunkenness, fighting, defamation, fornication, unchastity, cheating, stealing, idleness, [and] lying."[2]

Our initial response to this list is either to recoil in disgust at such narrow-mindedness or to smile and think, *How quaint.* In our grace-enlightened age, we know that judging others in the church is off-limits. After all, didn't Jesus say, "Do not judge so that you will not be judged" (Matthew 7:1)? To insist on standards of belief and behavior in a congregation would only reinforce the negative perceptions non-Christians have of the church—or so we think. We assume that encouraging Christians to correct fellow believers when they stray is the antithesis of grace. We fear that if we take discipline to the extreme and actually expel unrepentant members, we risk a church split or a lawsuit.

Why are we so reluctant to confront those in the church who are living in sexual immorality, teaching false doctrine, or threatening the unity of the congregation? Some suggest that the consumer mentality many Christians embrace regarding the church makes discipline difficult. Haddon Robinson, president of Denver Conservative Baptist Theological Seminary, observes,

> Too often now when people join a church, they do so as consumers. If they like the product, they stay. If they do not, they leave. They can no more imagine a church disciplining them than they could a store that sells goods disciplining them. It is not the place of the seller to discipline the consumer.[3]

The unspoken fear of many church leaders is that, given the shopper mentality of many believers, the practice of church discipline will keep potential members away from the church, drive current members out of the church, or cause serious division within the church.

Others are reluctant to practice church discipline because of bad examples they have witnessed in the past. When I served as an associate to the late Dr. W. A. Criswell of the historic First Baptist Church in Dallas, I asked him one day why the church did not deal firmly with errant members. He replied, "Robert, when I was a boy, I remember attending a service in which a man was brought before the congregation and disciplined by the leaders of the church. The words that were spoken were filled with harshness and hatred. Even though I was just a child, I remember thinking to myself that the ones doing the discipline were in more need of correction than the one being disciplined." But as one writer observed, "The answer to bad church discipline is good church discipline, not no church discipline."[4]

Perhaps the major reason we refuse to correct other believers is our failure to understand the responsibility we have toward each other in the church. When we become members of a local congregation, we are not joining a club; we are being added to a body of believers.

When you join a club you retain a large degree of anonymity. The only time you see other club members is at the prescribed time of the meetings. Even then, there is little interaction between members of the club. Rarely does conversation with other club members stray from superficial comments or issues related directly to the club. Someone in a stamp collectors' club would never think of asking about the state of another member's finances or inquiring about the health of someone else's marriage. As Dr. John White notes, the philosophy of a club is "live and let live."[5]

But the "live and let live" philosophy doesn't work in a body. All the parts of a body are vitally connected to one another. If there is a tumor on the pancreas, the liver cannot say, "Well, I'm sorry the pancreas is sick, but that's not my problem." As the pancreas goes, so goes the rest of the body. Or as Paul wrote,

> If one member suffers, all the members suffer with it; if one member is honored, all the members rejoice with it. Now you are Christ's body, and individually members of it. (1 Corinthians 12:26-27)

When you become a Christian, not only are you joined together with Jesus Christ (the Head); you are also joined together with all other Christians on earth as well as with those in heaven. This "body" is known as the church of Jesus Christ. But as we saw in chapter 9, God's plan for you is to also become a member of a local group of believers who have organized themselves to fulfill the Great Commission to "make disciples" of Jesus Christ (Matthew 28:19-20).

How does a local church fulfill Christ's mandate to make disciples? Certainly evangelism is an important component. Sharing the good news of God's grace ministers to those outside the church so that they might be freed from the bondage of sin. However, once those on the outside the church become part of the fellowship in the church, they need to grow in their relationship to Christ. Many within local fellowships still find themselves prisoners of greed, lust, ambition, gluttony, or some other sin that strangles their relationship with God.

That is where correction comes in. As one writer notes, church discipline is really a corollary of evangelism. "In discipline, as in the presentation of the good news to the non-Christian, a person is presented the opportunity of being liberated from the power of sin in all its forms by coming under the rule of Christ and walking in His way."[6]

Evangelism and church discipline are different strategies to accomplish the same goal: producing a group of men and women—disciples—who live under the rule of Jesus Christ. Evangelism focuses on freeing *unbelievers* from sin, while discipline focuses on the liberation of *fellow believers* from sin.

What Is Discipline?

J. Carl Laney offers this simple definition of church discipline: "the confrontive and corrective measures taken by an individual, church leaders, or the congregation regarding a matter of sin in the life of a believer."[7]

This kind of confrontation and correction, when performed the right way, is a demonstration of love, not hatred. For example, suppose in a routine exam your physician discovers a lump on your arm. Further tests reveal that the lump is a malignant tumor that threatens your life. But your doctor chooses to keep the results from you, reasoning to himself, "Surgery is painful, and it would be unloving to cut into another person's body" or "I don't want to take the risk inherent in surgery" or "Maybe I should just hope the problem heals itself" or "Who am I to judge someone else's health?"

Any of those excuses would be grounds for a malpractice suit! Yes, surgery is painful, but at times it is also necessary in order to bring healing.

Similarly, as members of the same spiritual body, we have a responsibility to help restore the spiritual health of those fellow members of the body who become infected with sin:

> If your brother sins, go and show him his fault in private; if he
> listens to you, you have won your brother. (Matthew 18:15)

> Do you not judge those who are within the church? But those who
> are outside, God judges. Remove the wicked man from among
> yourselves. (1 Corinthians 5:12-13)

> If anyone does not obey our instruction in this letter, take special
> note of that person and do not associate with him, so that he will
> be put to shame. Yet do not regard him as an enemy, but admonish
> him as a brother. (2 Thessalonians 3:14-15)

If any among you strays from the truth and one turns him back, let him know that he who turns a sinner from the error of his way will save his soul from death and will cover a multitude of sins. (James 5:19-20)

Discipline is a sign of love, not contempt for another person. The writer of Hebrews, quoting from the Old Testament, reminds us that it is because of God's love for us, not His hatred of us, that He corrects us:

Do not regard lightly the discipline of the Lord,
Nor faint when you are reproved by Him;
For those whom the Lord loves He disciplines,
And He scourges every son whom He receives. (Hebrews 12:5-6)

In fact, the writer goes on to argue, God's correction is evidence that we really are part of His family:

If you are without discipline, of which all have become partakers,
then you are illegitimate children and not sons. (Hebrews 12:8)

The only people God disciplines are those who are part of His family. For example, if you were at a shopping mall and heard a child screaming obscenities, chances are you would not attempt to correct him. If you tried, the child (or parent) would probably respond, "Who do you think you are?" Parents only discipline their own children, not someone else's children. It is part of their family responsibility.

Similarly, in the church we have a family responsibility for the spiritual health of the church as a whole as well as the individual members of the church. Disciplining other believers within the church accomplishes three major objectives.

The Purposes of Church Discipline

First, *discipline is necessary to restore a Christian who has been overtaken by sin.* My first dramatic role was that of the good Samaritan in our first-grade Sunday-school class. Even those with only a superficial acquaintance with the Bible know the basic plot of the story Jesus told in Luke 10.

In answer to an attorney who was looking for a loophole in the "love your neighbor as yourself" command, Jesus answered his question, "Who is my neighbor?" with a story. A band of robbers ambushed an Israelite traveling by foot and left him for dead. A priest and then a Levite (an assistant priest) walked by without offering the victim any help. However, a man from Samaria stopped and rendered aid to the Israelite and then paid for his recuperation at a nearby inn. The irony of the story is that Samaritans and Jews hated one another. The phrase *good Samaritan* was an oxymoron to Jews—much like "good terrorist" would be for us today.

On a deeper level, this parable reminded Jesus's listeners that Judaism, as practiced by the Pharisees, was bankrupt in its ability to offer genuine help for those in the world who had been attacked, beaten, and left for dead by sin. It would take an outsider to come and offer true healing. Jesus, of course, was that Outsider who provides what religion could never offer.

But apart from this deeper Christological significance, just a casual reading of the story teaches that passing by another person in need is cruel and unloving, which is why many states have adopted good Samaritan laws, giving legal protection to those who stop and render aid to accident victims. Our society deems it important to encourage its citizens to help those who are in distress.

The same principle applies to those we encounter who have been assaulted by sin. To ignore a fellow believer who is allowing immorality, dishonesty, or addiction to destroy his or her life is cruel. To use grace as an excuse for not rescuing another Christian from the Enemy's grip is to make a mockery of the word. "Reproof is a Christian duty," evangelist Charles Finney once remarked. "If you see your neighbor sin and you pass by and neglect to reprove him, it is just as cruel as if you should see his house on fire and pass by and not warn him of it."[8]

One reason so many people react negatively to the idea of church discipline is the erroneous assumption that the major motivation behind it is condemnation. However, restoration, not condemnation, should be the impetus for correcting another believer, as Paul reminded the Galatians:

> If anyone is caught in any trespass, you who are spiritual, restore such a one in a spirit of gentleness; each one looking to yourself, so that you too will not be tempted. (Galatians 6:1)

The word translated "restore" *(katartizō)* means "to repair or restore something to its previous condition." Often this word was used to describe the mending of a fishing net that had been torn or the setting of a fractured bone so that it might be healed. In both instances, the emphasis is on repairing something that is broken. The apostle Paul employed this word to remind us of our duty to help restore a life that has been broken by sin. Whenever a fellow believer is caught or trapped in a sin, we have a duty to help rescue and restore that person. It is the loving thing to do.

Second, *discipline is necessary to maintain the witness of the church.* As the body of Christ, Christians are the visible representation of Jesus Christ to the world. A non-Christian's attitude toward Jesus is largely influenced by his or her attitude toward those who claim to be His followers. When a non-Christian sees little difference in the morality, business ethics, response to tragedy, or attitudes of Christians compared to non-Christians, what motivation does that person have to take up his or her cross and follow Christ? Why bother?

Several nights ago I watched Larry King interview a well-known Christian entertainer who had divorced her husband to marry a man who was also married. Throughout the broadcast, this caption appeared under their image: "Christians attracted to each other while married to other people." The message that this entertainer was sending to millions of unbelievers was more powerful than all of her songs combined. If Christians don't live any differently than anyone else, then why bother? Or, as Gandhi once observed, "I might become a Christian, if I ever met one."

Christians entangled in sin have been a hindrance to Christianity since the earliest days of the church. A sex scandal brewing in the church at Corinth was the talk of the entire community. A member of the congregation was having an affair with his stepmother. Yet the church was unwilling to deal with the problem. If we read between the lines of 1 Corinthians 5, it appears that the church leaders actually prided themselves on their non-judgmental attitude. "Our church is built on grace. We don't judge other people. Everyone is welcome in our congregation," church leaders were apparently boasting.

But when the apostle Paul heard about the problem, he lambasted the leaders for refusing to deal with a sin so heinous that even unbelievers shook their heads in disgust when they heard of it:

> You have become arrogant and have not mourned instead, so that
> the one who had done this deed would be removed from your
> midst. (1 Corinthians 5:2)

Too often the church focuses on the misbehavior of non-Christians rather than that of believers. We rail against homosexuality, the lottery, abortion, pornography, and other symptoms of a society in rebellion against God. (Confession: I have done my share of railing as well). Yet, Paul reminded the Corinthians that it is God's job to police the activities of unbelievers. It is the church's job to clean up the sin in its own backyard:

What have I to do with judging outsiders? Do you not judge those who are within the church? But those who are outside, God judges. Remove the wicked man from among yourselves. (1 Corinthians 5:12-13)

As I have recounted in my book *Hell? Yes!* some years ago our church took a strong stand against two pro-homosexual books in the children's section of our local library. For weeks our local newspaper and news broadcasts were dominated by coverage of the controversy our church had generated. However, during this period of time one of our church leaders became involved in a relationship with another man's wife. I'll admit that it was tempting to sweep the problem under the rug. After all, what if the information became public? Our church would be humiliated, and more important, the cause of Christ would be harmed.

Fortunately, a group of leaders in our church reminded me of the consequences of not dealing with this problem. They pointed out that more than likely the information about the leader was already being whispered about in the community. Not dealing with problems with our own members while chastising the immoral practices of unbelievers would be the height of hypocrisy. So we confronted and corrected the leader, using the steps we will examine in the next chapter. Some time after that, a woman (not a member of our congregation) stopped me on the street and said, "I was just waiting to see if you people down at First Baptist Church were really going to practice what you preach." Fortunately, in this case we did.

A final reason for exercising discipline is to *sustain the health of the entire congregation.* You've heard the expression "One bad apple spoils the entire barrel." In Paul's day there was a similar saying: "A little leaven leavens the whole lump of dough" (1 Corinthians 5:6). Leaven is an important ingredient in the baking process. Just as it only took a little pinch of leaven to make a whole batch of dough rise, Paul said it takes only a little bit of sin to permeate and contaminate an entire congregation.

Paul then extended the analogy, alluding to an Old Testament practice:

Clean out the old leaven so that you may be a new lump, just as you are in fact unleavened. For Christ our Passover also has been sacrificed. (1 Corinthians 5:7)

If all this talk of leaven, baking, and dough seems foreign to you because you are as culinarily challenged as I am, a little background material might be helpful. Before God sent the tenth and final plague on Egypt to persuade Pharaoh to release the Israelites, the Lord instructed every Israelite to place the blood of a spotless lamb on the doorposts of each home. When God passed through the streets of Egypt to kill the firstborn of every home, He "passed over" the homes where the blood was applied. From that moment in history until the present, Jews commemorate that night by celebrating Passover.

The death of Pharaoh's own son that night was the final straw. He ordered the Israelites to leave Egypt immediately. In fact, they left in such a hurry that they took their dough with them before it was leavened. As a reminder of that experience, the Jews had a custom of lighting a candle and going through their home looking for any traces of leaven before they would sit down and enjoy the Passover meal. Why? Leaven represented their way of life in Egypt and was equated with sin. Now that they had been liberated from Egypt to a new way of life, sin had no place in their new existence.

Of course, the Passover lamb that was offered that first night—and every year since that time—represents Jesus Christ, the true Lamb of God. When we trust Him for our salvation, God's judgment passes over us, and He offers us a new life.

But with God's gift of forgiveness comes the responsibility to live distinctively. Sin has no place in our lives individually or in our collective lives as the body of Christ:

> Let us celebrate the feast, not with old leaven, nor with the leaven of malice and wickedness, but with the unleavened bread of sincerity and truth. (1 Corinthians 5:8)

Just as every Israelite family was to sweep away any leaven from their home, so every Christian is to carefully look for and remove any traces of sin from his or her life.

But the emphasis in this passage is on dealing with sin corporately, not individually. In 1 Corinthians 5:7, Paul's command to "clean out the old leaven" is a call not only to personal holiness but also to congregational holiness. The phrase "a new lump" refers to an entire congregation. The Corinthians' unwillingness to deal decisively with the immoral man within their congregation threatened to contaminate the entire church. After all, it takes only a little leaven to affect the whole lump.

Does this mean that we are to confront and correct every sin—no matter how seemingly inconsequential—in the church? If so, won't discipline become the overriding emphasis of the church? Do we really want to be part of a fellowship that expends all its energy focusing on other people's foibles?

Scriptural instruction, coupled with common sense, provides some practical answers to the questions "When should we correct another Christian?" and "How do I confront another person without doing irreparable harm?"

The answers to these questions is the focus of the next chapter.

CHAPTER TWELVE

Good Grace
Spiritual Surgery

Tamara, I thought you should know that I overheard Rhonda criticizing you—especially the way you dress—in front of some of the women in our small group," Patty informed her best friend. Since Rhonda had never voiced her concerns to Tamara personally, she was clearly guilty of gossip. Should Tamara confront Rhonda directly about her "sin"? If Rhonda is unrepentant, should she follow the steps outlined in Matthew 18 and take several more people to talk to Rhonda? If she still refuses to acknowledge her sin, should the leaders of the church expel Rhonda from the congregation? Or should Tamara simply forgive Rhonda and move on?

In the previous chapter we discussed the three major purposes of confronting and correcting a fellow Christian who sins. But the challenging question is "When should I confront another person about an offense, and when should I just let it go?"

Answering the "When" Question

I believe the Bible indicates that the degree to which we confront another Christian should be determined by the kind of offense committed.

Personal Offenses Against Us

It is only natural that the people we are most interested in reproving are those who hurt us. Don, the church member in the previous chapter who had been cheated out of twenty thousand dollars, wanted church discipline in-stituted against the fraudulent elder because of a loss Don had person-ally suffered. He cited the procedure for church discipline that Jesus out-lined in Matthew 18 as a rationale for removing the elder from the congregation if necessary.

However, Don should have read a little farther in Matthew 18. Jesus made a clear delineation between those who sin and those who sin against *us*. In Matthew 18 Jesus discussed our responsibility to fellow Christians who are entangled in sin. He compared the believer who is overtaken by sin to a stray sheep that has wandered away from the fold:

> What do you think? If any man has a hundred sheep, and one of
> them has gone astray, does he not leave the ninety-nine on the moun-
> tains and go and search for the one that is straying? If it turns out
> that he finds it, truly I say to you, he rejoices over it more than over
> the ninety-nine which have not gone astray. (Matthew 18:12-13)

Although many use this passage to illustrate God's concern for unbe-lievers, a closer reading of the text reveals that Jesus was really talking about God's concern for disobedient Christians. The one sheep that has strayed away from the shepherd is a legitimate member of the flock, not a kanga-roo or a wolf in sheep's clothing. The only reason the shepherd seeks to find and return the lost sheep to the safety of the sheepfold is because that is where the sheep belongs.

Jesus was saying that we should demonstrate the same concern for other Christians who stray from the Shepherd:

If your brother sins, go and show him his fault in private; if he lis-
tens to you, you have won your brother. (Matthew 18:15)

If he doesn't respond, Jesus gave additional steps we are to take to
restore a brother or sister who has strayed. A true follower of Christ will
display the same attitude toward errant believers as Jesus did. We will do
whatever is necessary to engage in a search-and-rescue mission to return
them to the safety of God's care and rule over their lives.

After Jesus's words about discipline and restoration, Peter asked a natural follow-up question: "Lord, how often shall my brother sin *against me*
and I forgive him?" (Matthew 18:21).

Although some translations omit the words "against me," it is still clear
that Peter was changing the topic from a *sinning* Christian to an *offending*
Christian. When a fellow Christian wrongs us, the only appropriate response
is to forgive him or her.

But aren't Christians who slander us, cheat us, or mistreat us also in
need of correction? If we forgive them without correcting them, aren't we
hurting them as well as the church?

Yes, those who sin against us do need to be reproved—but preferably
by *someone else*. For example, it might be entirely appropriate for Tamara to
confront Rhonda about the malicious gossip, as long as Tamara's primary
motivation is to help restore Rhonda or to clear the air in order to rebuild
their relationship. On the other hand, Don's apparent motivation for disciplining the cheating elder was to get his "pound of flesh" by having the
elder removed from the fellowship.

In the arena of personal offenses, we should always forgive and sometimes even reprove our offender. But beyond a private conversation with
the person, we should leave the more serious steps of correction to someone else, such as a friend or a church leader.

Personal Sins in Others

The second category of transgressions to consider are sins we observe in someone else's life. For example, if you encounter a fellow Christian who has allowed immorality, greed, anger, or some other sin to overtake him, then you have a family responsibility to help rescue him from that sin. I believe the apostle James had this category of sin in mind when he wrote,

> If any among you strays from the truth and one turns him back, let him know that he who turns a sinner from the error of his way will save his soul from death and will cover a multitude of sins. (James 5:19-20)

James said nothing about a congregational meeting in which the sinning believer is turned out of the church. Such a severe action may be necessary for some sins, but not for every sin. Instead, James portrayed a believer who, out of concern for a sinning believer's spiritual health, privately confronts him or her about harmful actions or attitudes.

Depending on the severity of the actions or the attitude of the one being confronted, you may need the assistance of several Christians in your rescue effort. Paul described this scenario in Galatians 6:

> If anyone is caught in any trespass, you who are spiritual, restore such a one in a spirit of gentleness; each one looking to yourself, so that you too will not be tempted. (verse 1)

Notice that Paul said nothing about turning the sinning believer out of the church as Jesus described in Matthew 18, or as Paul himself prescribed for the man sleeping with his stepmother in 1 Corinthians 5. The inference is that some offenses do not demand the ultimate penalty of excommunication from a fellowship.

Then when *should* the church go to the final step of actually dismissing someone from the fellowship of the church?

Corporate Sins Against the Church

Admittedly, some Christians believe that all the steps of discipline, including revocation of church membership, should be followed for every sin. During the Reformation, Martin Luther advocated excommunicating a man who sold a home for 400 guilders that he had purchased for 30 guilders. Luther felt that 150 guilders was the proper selling price and that by asking more, the seller was guilty of greed and in need of discipline.

Even today some suggest that we should have a no-tolerance policy for sin. No matter how seemingly insignificant an offense may be, they argue, it is enough to destroy the purity of a church. One pastor argues persuasively for such a stance:

> The New Testament teaches that no sin is tolerable to those whom Christ has redeemed. No Christian should be allowed to embrace unrepented sin and move in and out of the church at will.
>
> Difficult as it may be, the contemporary church must follow the mandate that any sin, whether seemingly insignificant (gluttony) or harsh (incest), must be approached in the spirit of Christ. Recognizing this responsibility will propel the church into a regular program of discipline.[1]

While I agree with the author that all sin is serious, we must step back for a moment and ask ourselves if we really want to start holding congregational meetings to expel a member from the fellowship because he or she has made too many trips to Burger King. Admittedly, lack of control over one's appetite has serious ramifications for a person's health, the welfare of his or her family, and perhaps that person's witness to unbelievers. However, aren't such "sins" better handled by one or two concerned friends gently offering to help the bloated believer gain control over his or her weight?

The Scriptures indicate that while not every sin must be dealt with publicly, there are at least three instances in which the seriousness of the offense so damages the congregation that it must be publicly confronted if the offender is unwilling to repent.

1. Sins that threaten the moral health of the church. A church member who engages in sexual immorality or financial dishonesty compromises the church's witness to unbelievers in the community by weakening its moral authority. More times than I wish to remember, I have heard comments from non-Christians, such as "I can't believe you allow _____ to be a member of your church. Do you know what he is doing?" These comments are then followed by some sordid tale of financial or sexual mischief.

Overt sins that are not corrected, such as immorality and financial impropriety, not only *affect* those outside the church, they also *infect* those within the church. When congregational leaders refuse to deal with these sins that are also well known within the congregation, they are implicitly approving such offenses. "A little leaven leavens the whole lump of dough." In the case of the immoral Corinthian who was having an open affair with his stepmother, Paul commanded his removal not only to maintain the church's witness but also to restore the church's moral health.

2. Sins that threaten the doctrinal health of the church. In my first pastorate I was informed that a youth Sunday-school teacher had discarded our curriculum and was teaching on the relationship between Halley's comet and the second coming of Christ. I met with her privately and asked her to cease and desist, but she continued to teach her special series of lessons. Eventually, the leaders of the church removed her from her position.

While her teaching was questionable, it probably did not warrant her removal from the church. However, Scripture indicates some doctrinal errors are so serious that they cannot be tolerated. Any false teaching concerning the deity of Christ, the means of salvation, or the authority of Scripture must be dealt with firmly. Paul commanded Timothy, the pastor of the church in Ephesus, to deal decisively with those who promote false doctrine:

> If any man teach otherwise, and consent not to wholesome words,
> even the words of our Lord Jesus Christ, and to the doctrine which
> is according to godliness; he is proud, knowing nothing, but doting
> about questions and strifes of words, whereof cometh envy, strife,
> railings, evil surmisings, perverse disputings of men of corrupt
> minds, and destitute of the truth, supposing that gain is godliness:
> *from such withdraw thyself.* (1 Timothy 6:3-5, KJV)

Tolerating a diversity of views within the church on essential doctrines is bad grace at its worst. Failure to correct and, if necessary, remove a false teacher brings God's judgment against any congregation.

Remember God's indictment against the church at Thyatira? Not wanting to be seen as overly dogmatic and harsh, the leaders of the church allowed a woman to continue promoting false doctrine. "Who are we to judge? Shouldn't everyone be allowed to interpret Scripture for themselves?" they rationalized. But God viewed their failure to act as a weakness, not a strength:

> I have this against you, that you tolerate the woman Jezebel, who
> calls herself a prophetess, and she teaches and leads My bond-
> servants astray so that they commit acts of immorality and eat
> things sacrificed to idols. (Revelation 2:20)

God has a zero-tolerance policy for false teaching within the church. And so should we.

3. Sins that threaten the emotional health of the church. Although we tend to think of gossip, slander, criticism, and other sins of the tongue as minor

infractions since "everybody does it," such offenses can have major consequences within a church fellowship. "See how great a forest is set aflame by
such a small fire!" James 3:5 warns. It takes only a few unguarded comments to generate a firestorm of controversy that can consume an entire
congregation.

I continually remind our members, especially our leaders, that they will encounter frequent "sparks" of controversy as they move about the congregation.

"Did you hear what the pastor did last week?"

"Do you feel like our church is moving in the right direction?"

"I'm concerned that our worship services are becoming too entertainment oriented."

When leaders hear such comments, they can throw either water or
kerosene on the spark. Such responses as "I think you misunderstood what he
said," "Why don't we pray about this rather than criticize?" or "Have you spoken privately to the person responsible for this?" have a way of immediately
quenching the controversy. However, agreeing with such criticisms—either
by our words, facial expressions, or silence—only adds fuel to the spark.

God calls us to be firefighters rather than fire starters in the church. We
are to be vigilant against anyone or anything that would disrupt the unity
of our fellowship. "[Be] diligent to preserve the unity of the Spirit in the
bond of peace," Paul urged the Christians at Ephesus (Ephesians 4:3). That
duty sometimes involves removing from the rest of the congregation those
who continually generate sparks of controversy.

> Now I urge you...keep your eye on those who cause dissensions and
> hindrances contrary to the teaching which you learned, and turn
> away from them. (Romans 16:17)

Some time ago a leader in our congregation was continually causing a
stir within the fellowship. He was constantly calling other members and

voicing his "concern" about various staff members and spreading false information about the church finances. Fortunately, Paul's words to Titus gave us the courage we needed to confront the situation:

> Reject a factious man after a first and second warning, knowing
> that such a man is perverted and is sinning, being self-condemned.
> (Titus 3:10-11)

While removing such a member from leadership was risky, Paul understood that allowing him to remain was even more dangerous.

But how do we go about correcting another Christian without doing irreparable harm to that person or to the congregation? As we saw, the word *restore* in Galatians 6:1 was used in Greek medical texts to describe setting a fractured bone. Any kind of surgery is risky, especially surgery on something as delicate as a person's soul. The success of surgery depends largely on the skill of the surgeon. Perhaps you feel a little shaky about performing such a procedure on another Christian. After all, you haven't attended medical school (a.k.a. seminary) to become equipped to deal with such matters.

But Jesus did not restrict such operations to the paid professionals. Instead, all of us have a responsibility to help remove the tumor of sin from a fellow believer's life, and Jesus gave us the procedure to follow.

A GUIDEBOOK TO SPIRITUAL SURGERY

In Matthew 18, Jesus outlined the steps we are to take in confronting another believer who has been overtaken by sin.

1. Talk with the person privately. Here's the major difference between condemnation and restoration. Those who simply want to condemn others— usually for the sake of elevating themselves—will deal as publicly as possible with the sinner. But someone who is truly interested in restoring a fellow

Christian will deal with the situation as privately as possible. For that reason, Jesus said,

> If your brother sins, go and show him his fault *in private;*
> if he listens to you, you have won your brother. (Matthew
> 18:15)

The term Jesus used for sin *(harmartia)* means "to miss the mark." Anytime we see a fellow believer who is missing the mark in relation to God's standard for any area of life, we have a responsibility to gently offer a word of correction. All the categories of sin discussed in the previous section—such as personal offenses, personal sins, and corporate sins—would warrant this kind of one-on-one reproof.

However, if a fellow Christian's sin falls under the category of a personal offense—that is, a sin against us, personally—we must make sure we have truly forgiven the person before we seek to restore him or her. Otherwise, our true motive may be revenge rather than restoration. Frankly, since very few of us (including myself) have the ability to be objective enough to lay aside our personal feelings when confronting someone who has wronged us, this kind of operation is best left to another Christian.

While we don't need a seminary degree to perform such a procedure, we must meet one qualification: Those offering correction must already have dealt with sin in their own lives. In an earlier passage in Matthew, Jesus instructed,

> Do not judge so that you will not be judged. For in the way you
> judge, you will be judged; and by your standard of measure, it will
> be measured to you...You hypocrite, first take the log out of your
> own eye, and then you will see clearly to take the speck out of your
> brother's eye. (7:1-2,5)

Those under the influence of bad grace would use this verse as an excuse to shirk their responsibility to correct a fellow believer. But closer examination of the word Jesus used for "judge" reveals that He was referring to a condemning kind of final judgment that only God can perform— a pronouncement that says someone is beyond redemption. The motive for this kind of judgment, which the Pharisees routinely practiced, is to elevate one's own goodness above that of others. However, the succeeding verses reveal that Jesus was not prohibiting all kinds of judgment. He went ahead to explain how to "take the speck out of your brother's eye" (verse 5). He instructs us to remove the sin ("log") from our own lives so that we may see clearly to remove the sin from another believer's life.

This doesn't mean we must be perfect before we can correct another Christian. However, Jesus's words do require us to have dealt as decisively as possible with any obvious areas of disobedience in our own life before we attempt to correct someone else. Otherwise, it is as if we are attempting to perform surgery blindfolded. In that situation, neither the patient nor the doctor feels confident!

If our fellow believer responds to our correction, then we have "won" our brother. The word translated "won" means "to accumulate wealth." One more of God's sheep has been returned to the fold, and that constitutes a "win" for us. At that point we are to drop the matter. No further action is necessary. But what if the sinning believer refuses to listen to correction and continues in his or her disobedience?

2. Take a small group with you to talk with the person. Jesus realized that there would be times when a disobedient Christian would not respond to private correction, so He gave this instruction:

If he [the disobedient Christian] does not listen to you, take one or two more with you, so that by the mouth of two or three witnesses every fact may be confirmed. (Matthew 18:16)

What is the purpose of taking two or three other Christians with you to talk with the disobedient believer? Some have suggested that these are people who have witnessed the same offense that demands correction. Yet, rarely do such eyewitnesses exist. More likely, the reason for taking several people along is so that the offending believer will realize that this is more than a personal vendetta you have against him or her. Also, if the person still refuses to listen to the correction, the other people present can confirm his or her unrepentant attitude to church leaders should further action be warranted.

Whether we are meeting privately or in a small group with a Christian who is caught up in sin, it is imperative that we do so "in a spirit of gentleness" (Galatians 6:1). After all, a successful surgeon uses a scalpel, not a pickax, to perform a delicate procedure. That means we should refrain from harsh words and reaffirm our desire for the person's restoration.

But what if the disobedient believer persists in disobedience and tells the group who is confronting him or her to mind their own business? Jesus knew that was a distinct possibility, so He provided us with the next step of action.

3. Report the situation to the congregation. After a reasonable period of time has elapsed for the sinning Christian to consider the private rebuke he or she has received, Jesus said that it is time to take the offense public if the person remains unrepentant: "If he [the unrepentant believer] refuses to listen to them [those who have confronted him privately], tell it to the church" (Matthew 18:17).

The purpose of reporting the sin to the church is not to humiliate the person. Instead, the congregation is informed so that the members might pray for his or her repentance and also be prepared for the next, most extreme step of action, should it be required.

It is important to pause here and observe that Jesus was giving us general guidelines, not detailed instructions, for how to handle sin in the church. The number of unanswered questions that arise from this passage indicate to me that Jesus gave us great latitude in how to apply these principles, depending on the individual situation.

For example, since Jesus never precisely described the kind of sin that would require this more drastic action, leaders may exercise discernment in deciding which sins need to be made public. I personally believe that the third and fourth steps of action Jesus outlined should be reserved for corporate sins—sins that threaten the moral, doctrinal, or emotional health of the entire congregation.

Furthermore, the command to "tell it to the church" may involve telling the elders or a small group of leaders rather than making a public announcement on Sunday morning. Remember, these instructions are not an end unto themselves; they are the means to an end: the restoration of a sinning believer. Making public the habits of a Christian who is guilty of gluttony or addicted to pornography will probably do more harm than good to both the believer and the congregation. Jesus expects us to use good judgment instead of following the letter of the law here.

4. If necessary, remove the believer from the congregation. In extreme instances, an unrepentant Christian must be removed from the congregation.

> If he refuses to listen even to the church, let him be to you as a
> Gentile and a tax collector. (Matthew 18:17)

Some commentators, like William Barclay, refuse to believe that Jesus actually spoke these words because they lack the "charity and forgiveness" that were characteristic of Jesus's other teachings.[2] Such a charge is based on the false assumption that love and discipline are mutually exclusive. Yet sometimes we must take severe measures to restore a Christian, even if those measures cause temporary discomfort. A surgeon has to cut in order to heal.

There are two reasons for removing a sinning Christian from the fellowship of a church and treating him or her as an outsider (or as Jesus said, "a Gentile and a tax collector"). Revoking the person's membership will serve as a wake-up call to the seriousness of the offense and will hopefully lead to his or her repentance and restoration. Also, removing the unrepentant believer from the church will protect the spiritual, moral, and emotional health of the fellowship, as in the case of the Corinthian who was living with his stepmother.

Again, it should be pointed out that the only time the New Testament records this extreme action being taken is in the case of overt sin that threatened the well-being of an entire congregation, such as the situation in the Corinthian church.

But Does It *Really* Work?

I have noticed that many pastors who either teach or write on the subject of church discipline rarely practice it in their own congregations. For the purpose of full disclosure, I should inform you that I have regularly practiced the first three steps Jesus outlined here, but I have never been involved in revoking someone's church membership (although I have refused membership to some people who I feared would threaten the health of the congregation). Furthermore, my "success rate" in restoring believers is nothing to brag about. Many times the person I attempt to restore becomes angry and moves to another church without my having to resort to the final two steps Jesus outlined in Matthew 18.

But sometimes church discipline does work. The church leaders in Corinth apparently took Paul's rebuke seriously and removed the immoral member from their congregation. According to 2 Corinthians 2:6-8, the sinning believer eventually repented, and Paul urged the Corinthians to receive him back into the fellowship.

The principles Jesus and Paul outlined still work today. When the late Ray Stedman, pastor of Peninsula Bible Church in Palo Alto, California, and the leaders of his church became aware of a member's homosexual practices, they went through the steps of spiritual surgery discussed in this chapter. At first the member did not respond positively. However, five years later he wrote a letter to the church, thanking the leaders for their courage in confronting his sin.

He wrote, "It is impossible for me to retrace my footsteps and right every wrong; however, I welcome the opportunity to meet and pray with any individuals who have something against me that needs resolution. I am looking and waiting for the further grace and mercy of God in this matter. What you have bound on earth has been bound in heaven, and I now know your actions were done in love for my own good and that of the body of Christ."[3]

In both surgery and discipline you lose some…but you also win some. And those wins make the process of restoration worthwhile.

Bad grace avoids the responsibility of discipline, resulting in an unhealthy congregation.

Good grace applies scriptural discipline in love, resulting in a healthier, happier, and more peaceful congregation.

Bad grace equates correction with condemnation.

Good grace understands that sometimes the most loving thing we can do for other believers is to confront them about their disobedience.

Bad grace uses the "live and let live" philosophy as an excuse for ignoring a fellow believer who is held hostage by sin.

Good grace recognizes that we have a responsibility to rescue other believers who have been overtaken by sin.

Bad grace rarely considers the effect that an individual's sin has on an entire congregation.

Good grace recognizes our responsibility to protect the moral, doctrinal, and emotional health of the church.

BALANCING
GOOD GRACE

CHAPTER THIRTEEN

Dancing on a Tightrope

When we think of the World Trade Center, we cannot help but re-member that awful autumn day in 2001 when terrorists crashed jetliners into the two skyscrapers, reducing them to a pile of rubble. But nearly thirty years earlier, the twin towers of the World Trade Center had been the site of another breathtaking occurrence.

At a few minutes past 7:00 a.m. on a late summer morning in 1974, one hundred thousand New Yorkers gazed a quarter-mile into the sky to watch a twenty-four-year-old high-wire artist named Philippe Petit make eight crossings on a cable stretched between the mammoth towers of the Trade Center. Petit's stunt was the culmination of six years of meticulous planning and rehearsal. The night before the stunt, Petit and six friends had clandestinely entered one of the towers and secured the 140-foot cable between the two buildings.

The next morning the slender Petit, dressed in black, stepped onto the cable, clutching a balancing pole. For the next forty-five minutes, Petit entertained the growing crowd below as angry law-enforcement officers scratched their heads and wondered how to stop him.

For variety, Petit would stop halfway between the towers and lie on his stomach or bend down on one knee as the audience gasped. "I could hear the horns of the cars below me," he recalled. "I could hear the applause, too. The *rumeur* (clamor) of the crowd rose up to me from 400 meters below. No other show person has ever heard a sound like that."[1]

When rain began to fall, Philippe Petit was forced to end his performance by running along the cable onto the landing of one of the towers—and into the arms of waiting New York City police officers. Petit became such an instant celebrity that law enforcement officials dropped charges against him, requiring only that he offer a free performance in Central Park the following weekend.

Later, the aerialist reflected on his emotions while walking on a thin wire between (at that time) the two highest structures in the world. "[At first] I felt fear, and I fought it, and then laughed at it. I...listened to the noises of the everyday world fall silent until I was surrounded by complete peace."[2]

Complete peace? Had the high altitude deprived Petit's brain of some much-needed oxygen? What could be more terrifying than carefully watching every step you take on a narrow cable strung more than one hundred stories in the air, knowing that the slightest deviation could send you to your death? But Petit knew that as long as he kept his balance, he was safe from any harm and free to enjoy the exhilarating experience for which he had spent years preparing.

"No sane person would attempt such a challenge," you might conclude. Yet, whether or not you realize it, you and I are performing our own spiritual balancing act. Every Christian walks a fine line between the twin towers of Freedom in Christ and Obedience to Christ. As we attempt to maintain our balance between grace and responsibility, the winds of criticism from others try to push us to one side or the other.

Whether we fall into legalism or libertarianism—which are both forms of bad grace—really doesn't matter. The results are equally lethal to our spiritual lives. Legalism leads to a sterile, ritualistic relationship with God, void of any joy. Libertarianism leads to disobedience that robs us of intimacy with God and its accompanying benefits.

Martin Luther once observed that the devil doesn't care which side of the horse we fall off, as long as we don't stay in the saddle. Fortunately, God has provided every Christian with a "balance bar" to help us navigate between the twin towers of freedom and obedience: It's called good grace. A proper understanding of God's greatest gift keeps us from falling into either extreme as we enjoy the freedom from condemnation that grace provides, while we remember the obligation to God and others that grace demands.

As we wrap up our discussion of good grace and bad grace, I would like to summarize by leaving you with three thoughts about good grace that will help you maintain your balance between freedom and obedience.

Good Grace Resists the Need to Judge Others

Yesterday a co-worker and I were discussing a prominent pastor and respected author who recently had fallen into immorality. The pastor was known primarily for his teaching on grace. Some who attended his congregation remarked to me that in the last year his teaching seemed increasingly unbalanced. He spoke almost incessantly about the freedom that grace provides, without mentioning the obedience that grace requires. "He needed a copy of your book," my staff members said. (My staff knows how to score points with the boss.) I'll admit the thought had also crossed my mind—and I imagine a similar thought has come to yours as well during this discussion. You can probably name several people right now who have perverted the doctrine of grace into an excuse for disobedience rather than seeing grace as an incentive for deeper faithfulness. They are using grace as a cover for immoral relationships, a self-centered lifestyle, or uninvolvement in God's kingdom. As we saw in the previous chapter, good grace recognizes

our responsibility to lovingly correct fellow believers who are living in blatant disobedience.

But many times we feel obligated to pass judgment on those whose
behavior, while not in violation of Scripture, violates our personal code of
conduct. Their actions fall in the gray areas we discussed in chapter 5. As
we observe people acting in a way we find objectionable, a righteous indignation wells up inside us. We feel overwhelmed by a desire to set them
straight. If we lack the courage to confront them directly, we don't hesitate
to criticize them privately. The apostle Paul offered three words to remember whenever that feeling overtakes us: *Stop judging others.*

That simple advice is the gist of Paul's counsel to the Christians in
Rome, recorded in Romans 14. Apparently the controversy over eating meat
offered to idols was not confined to the Corinthian church. The members
of the Roman church were also divided over that issue as well as many other
gray areas, such as the consumption of wine and the observance of the Sabbath. Their differences of opinion threatened to destroy the unity of their
congregation. With such divergent views, how could they ever hope to get
along with one another? In answer to that question, Paul wrote,

> The one who eats is not to regard with contempt the one who does
> not eat, and the one who does not eat is not to judge the one who
> eats, for God has accepted him. Who are you to judge the servant of
> another? To his own master he stands or falls; and he will stand, for
> the Lord is able to make him stand. (verses 3-4)

In other words, "Quit judging the person who doesn't see things the
way you do!" Why? First, Paul said, because "God has accepted him." This
is an amazingly simple, yet profound truth: God loves that Christian you
feel compelled to condemn as much as He loves you. That wine-drinking,
movie-going, Harry Potter–reading believer is just as much a part of God's

family as the teetotaling, cinema-abstaining, C. S. Lewis–only reading Christian. The reason we have difficulty believing that—*really* believing that—is because we create artificial divisions between people that God does not recognize.

Think for a moment about a great geological chasm such as the Grand Canyon. Many Christians want to place a similar divide between one another. But the real division is not between drinkers and abstainers, Calvinists and Arminians, fundamentalists and moderates, or premillennialists and amillennialists (if you aren't familiar with those terms, don't worry about it!). The only divide God recognizes is between those people who have received His amazing gift of grace and those who have rejected it: the saved and the lost. Because of grace, every Christian is on the same side of the great divide. Since God has accepted all believers—even those with whom we disagree—so should we.

Paul added an additional rationale for refusing to judge other Christians: If they are as wrong in their behavior as we think they are, God will judge them:

> Who are you to judge the servant of another? To his own master he stands or falls.... For we will all stand before the judgment seat of God. (Romans 14:4,10)

Imagine that I called the youth minister at another church in our city and said, "It has come to my attention that you sponsored a dance in your church's fellowship hall last Friday night, and I don't think that is right. I don't want to ever hear of you doing such a thing again." Within a few minutes I would probably receive a call from that church's pastor reading me the riot act: "Who do you think you are, reprimanding one of my staff members? You are not his pastor; I am! Mind your own business!"

Paul used the same analogy in Romans 14. With regard to the gray areas of life, why should we feel compelled to pass judgment on other Christians? They are not answerable to us for their behavior; they are answerable to God. If they are wrong, God will deal with them in this life, or at the Final Judgment.

Years ago a bus company had a slogan that went something like "Take the bus and leave the driving to us." Here's a slogan to remember the next time you feel the compulsion to judge another Christian with whom you disagree: "Don't be a clod; leave the judging to God."

Our primary responsibility is to focus on our own walk along the tightrope, making sure we do not fall into either legalism or libertarianism. To prevent such a fall, our balance bar needs to be equally weighted with grace on one end and responsibility on the other—which is why these next two principles are of equal importance.

GOOD GRACE REFUSES TO TRUST IN WORKS FOR SALVATION

I realize that some people might read the title of this book, skim the table of contents, look at the blurbs on the back cover, and conclude that this book is a thinly veiled attempt to place Christians under the yoke of legalism. Such skepticism is understandable. As one writer observed, for the past two thousand years, some have attempted to nail a sign to the Cross that reads "Necessary, But Not Enough." Their error is not in denying the necessity of Christ's death but in denying its sufficiency to completely cover our sins. And so salvation becomes a joint project between God and us. God supplies the grace, we supply the _____ (insert: baptism, church membership, tithing, keeping the Commandments, trying to be a good person, or whatever else you would like), and the result is eternal life.

But as we saw in chapter 3, trying to mix grace and works for salvation is like mixing oil and water. The two just don't go together. In Romans 4:4-5, Paul illustrated why grace and works are incompatible:

Now to the one who works, his wage is not credited as a favor, but as what is due. But to the one who does not work, but believes in Him who justifies the ungodly, his faith is credited as righteousness.

The Internal Revenue Service has a better understanding of these verses than many Christians. For example, pretend that out of the goodness of my heart, I give you ten thousand dollars. That gift is not reportable on your income-tax return because you did nothing to earn it. It was simply a gift.

But suppose I say to you, "I would like to give you ten thousand dollars, but I also need you to do something for me. In exchange for the money, would you paint my front door?" If you accepted the deal, you would have to report that money on your income-tax return because it was no longer a gift, but a wage for work performed.

"But wait a minute," you protest. "Painting a door is not worth ten thousand dollars! It's worth only five hundred dollars."

"Doesn't matter," says the IRS. "If you do *anything*—no matter how small—to earn that money, it is no longer a gift, but a wage."

God says the same thing about our salvation. If eternal life is 99 percent the result of God's grace and 1 percent dependent on our good works, then salvation is no longer a gift from God. It's a payment from God that we deserve. And God refuses to owe anyone salvation. Eternal life is either a gift or a wage; it cannot be both.

A few months ago I came across the best illustration of grace I have ever read. A ministerial student recalled a lesson about grace that she would never forget:

In the spring of 2002, I left work early so I could have some uninterrupted study time before my final exam in the Youth Ministry class at Hannibal-LaGrange college in Missouri. When I got to class, everybody was doing their last-minute studying. The teacher came in and said he would review with us before the test. Most of his review came right from the study guide, but there were some things he was reviewing that I had never heard. When questioned about it, he said they were in the book and we were responsible for every-thing in the book. We couldn't argue with that.

Finally it was time to take the test. "Leave them face down on the desk until everyone has one, and I'll tell you to start," our pro-fessor, Dr. Tom Hufty, instructed.

When we turned them over, to my astonishment every answer on the test was filled in. My name was even written on the exam in red ink. The bottom of the last page said: "This is the end of the exam. All the answers on your test are correct. You will receive an *A* on the final exam. The reason you passed the test is because the creator of the test took it for you. All the work you did in prepara-tion for this test did not help you get the *A*. You have just experi-enced...grace."

Dr. Hufty then went around the room and asked each student individually, "What is your grade? Do you deserve the grade you are receiving? How much did all your studying for this exam help you achieve your final grade?"

Then he said, "Some things you learn from lectures, some things you learn from research, but some things you can only learn from experience. You've just experienced grace. One hundred years from now, if you know Jesus Christ as your personal Savior, your name will be written down in a book, and you will have had nothing to do with writing it there. That will be the ultimate grace experience."[3]

Good grace understands that salvation is the result of what God has done for us, not what we have done for God.

But clinging to that truth alone makes us susceptible to falling into libertarianism. We need a complementary truth to maintain our spiritual balance.

GOOD GRACE RECOGNIZES OUR OBLIGATION TO OBEDIENCE

Author Dallas Willard identifies what I believe is the primary reason there is so little difference between the lifestyles of Christians and non-Christians. Many believers see their faith as no more than an effective sin-removal program that ensures that they make it to heaven when they die. Willard refers to such a system of belief as "bar-code" Christianity.

Today most products carry a bar code, which is read by a scanner at the checkout line. The scanner doesn't care what is inside the bottle or package to which the bar code is attached. If the bar code is mistakenly attached to a can of tuna fish instead of a carton of ice cream, the scanner "sees" the tuna fish as ice cream and registers the corresponding price.

In the same way, many Christians believe that once we trust in Christ for the forgiveness of our sins, God attaches a special bar code on our lives that reads "forgiven" and guarantees our entrance into heaven. God is not really concerned with the content of our lives, only that we carry the right "label."

While it is true that faith in Christ results in an immediate and irreversible change in our status from "condemned" to "forgiven," to say that God has no interest in the contents of the lives He went to the trouble of saving is absurd. As Willard reasons,

> Can we seriously believe that God would establish a plan for us that
> essentially bypasses the awesome needs of present human life and
> leaves human character untouched? Would he leave us even tem-
> porarily marooned with no help in our kind of world, with our

kinds of problems: psychological, emotional, social, and global? Can we believe that the essence of Christian faith and salvation covers nothing but death and after? Can we believe that being saved really has nothing whatever to do with the kinds of persons we are?[4]

When we receive God's gift of grace, He does provide us with a bar code that assures our entrance into heaven. The label reads "Jesus Christ." When we pass from this life into the next, the "divine scanner" in heaven registers our righteousness as being equal to that of Jesus Christ—all because of the price He paid on the cross.

But in addition to a new label, God also gives us a new Power who begins transforming us until what is inside us matches the label God has placed on us. Unlike our salvation, which is the result of God's work alone, this transformation of our actions, attitudes, and affections is a joint project between God's Holy Spirit and us—a process I detail in my book *I Want More!*

In Philippians 1:6, Paul wrote, "I am confident of this very thing, that He who began a good work in you will perfect it until the day of Christ Jesus."

Our cooperation in this transformation process is at the core of what it means to be Christ's disciple. Through the years I have read a multitude of definitions of the word *disciple,* but none is better than this one. Read this sentence very slowly: To be Christ's disciple means for me "to live my life as [Christ] would live my life if he were I."[5]

I have not been called to live the same life Jesus Christ lived. God did not place me in Israel during the first century to earn a living as a carpenter and offer my life for the sins of the world. Instead, he has called me to live in the twenty-first century as the husband of Amy Jeffress, father of Julia and Dorothy Jeffress, and pastor of the First Baptist Church in Wichita Falls, Texas. For me, being Christ's disciple means responding to Amy's needs this coming Saturday as Christ would if He were Amy's husband. It means answering my daughters' requests for help with their homework as Christ would if He were their father. It means having the same agenda at next Monday's staff meeting as Christ would if He were shepherding my congregation.

Obviously, pulling that off requires a radical change in my attitudes, affections, and actions. But God's gift of grace provides me with the power, the incentive, and, yes, the obligation to cooperate with Him in effecting that transformation.

After devoting the first three chapters of his letter to the Ephesian Christians to describing God's undeserved gift of grace, the apostle Paul spent the final three chapters outlining their obligation as a result of God's gift:

> I, the prisoner of the Lord, implore you to walk in a manner worthy of the calling with which you have been called. (Ephesians 4:1)

Grace Results in Both a Gift and an Obligation

Perhaps you saw the movie *Saving Private Ryan,* which tells the story of a group of GIs during World War II. The GIs, led by a captain (portrayed by Tom Hanks), have been ordered to rescue a private whose three brothers have already been killed. The soldiers complain about the unfairness and futility of the assignment as they face fierce opposition searching behind enemy lines for Private Ryan. Several of them lose their lives in the rescue attempt.

In the final scene of the movie, Private Ryan discovers the captain, who is lying on the ground mortally wounded. Ryan is visibly shaken as he comes to terms with the destruction that has occurred in the attempt to liberate him from enemy hands. The bloodied captain looks up at Ryan and says these final words: "Earn this."

How could Ryan earn his own rescue when he had nothing to do with it? A higher government power had ordered and executed the plan that would result in his deliverance from the enemy long before Ryan knew anything about it. But the private understood instantly what his captain meant. "You have been graced with the courage, the sacrifice, and finally the lives of those who died so that you might live.... You can live in a way that proves worthy of their sacrifices. Respond not out of guilt but out of gratitude, honoring what they have done."[6]

Before the foundation of the world, God conceived a plan to rescue you from the Enemy's grip. Two thousand years ago Jesus Christ willingly gave His life to execute that plan and secure your deliverance. Although there is nothing we can add to the sacrifice that has already been offered on our behalf, you and I can "walk in a manner worthy of the calling with which you have been called" (Ephesians 4:1).

Why would those of us who have been the recipients of God's good grace ever want to do anything less?

Notes

Chapter 1

1. This story originally appeared in Donald Grey Barnhouse, *How God Saves Men* (Philadelphia: The Bible Study Hour, 1955). My version is based on the story as told by James Montgomery Boice in *Romans: God and History*, vol. 3 (Grand Rapids: Baker Books, 1993), 1139-40. Also in James Montgomery Boice, *Ephesians: An Expositional Commentary* (Grand Rapids: Zondervan, 1988), 62-63.

2. See Charles R. Swindoll, *The Grace Awakening* (Nashville: W Publishing, 2003).

3. Paraphrased from Charles R. Swindoll, *Simple Faith* (Dallas: Word, 1991), xviii-xix.

4. Erwin W. Lutzer, *Your Eternal Reward: Triumph and Tears at the Judgment Seat of Christ* (Chicago: Moody Press, 1998), 72.

Chapter 2

1. John Newton, "Amazing Grace," 1779, public domain.

2. This illustration is from Harold S. Kushner, *When Bad Things Happen to Good People* (New York: HarperCollins, 1981), 61-62.

3. Based on Steve Farrar's illustration in *Gettin' There: How a Man Finds His Way on the Trail of Life* (Sisters, OR: Multnomah, 2001), 43.

4. See James Montgomery Boice, *Romans*, vol. 2 (Grand Rapids: Baker Books, 1992), 537.

5. Paraphrased from Larry Christianson, *The Renewed Mind* (Minneapolis: Bethany Fellowship, 1981), 41-42.

Chapter 3

1. Richard Mayhue, "Legalism: Does It Lead to True Righteousness," May-June 1998, www.ifca.org/voice/98May-Jun/Mayhue.htm.
2. Paraphrased from Tony Campolo, *The Kingdom of God is a Party* (Dallas: Word, 1990), 32-33.
3. Paraphrased from Randy Alcorn, *The Grace and Truth Paradox* (Sisters, OR: Multnomah, 2003), 79.
4. John MacArthur, "Obedience: Love or Legalism," (sermon, n.d.), www.biblebb.com/mac-h-z.htm.
5. Leroy Eims, "Why Obey God?" *Discipleship Journal,* vol. 6, no. 31 (January, 1986): 39.

Chapter 4

1. This story originally appeared in Sören Kierkegaard, *Philosophical Fragments,* trans. David Swenson (Princeton: Princeton University Press, 1962), 31-43. My version is based on Philip Yancey's paraphrase in *Disappointment with God: Three Questions No One Asks Aloud* (Grand Rapids: Zondervan, 1988), 103-4.
2. Simone Weil, *Gravity and Grace* (New York: Routledge, 1995), 62-63, quoted in Philip Yancey, *Rumors of Another World: What on Earth Are We Missing?* (Grand Rapids: Zondervan, 2003), 99.
3. Alan Redpath, *Victorious Christian Service: Studies in the Book of Nehemiah* (Westwood, NJ: Revell, 1958), 160.
4. Used by permission.
5. W. E. Vine, *Vine's Expository Dictionary of Old and New Testament Words* (Old Tappan, NJ: Revell, 1981), 2:71, quoted in John F. MacArthur, Jr., *The Gospel According to Jesus* (Grand Rapids: Zondervan, 1988), 174.
6. Charles R. Swindoll, *Becoming a People of Grace* (Plano, TX: Insight for Living, 2001), 57.

7. John Calvin, quoted in John Dillenberger, *John Calvin: Selections from His Writings* (New York: Oxford University Press, 1975), 198; John Piper, *Brothers, We Are Not Professionals: A Plea to Pastors for Radical Ministry* (Nashville: Broadman & Holman, 2002), 23.

8. Robert Jeffress, *As Time Runs Out* (Nashville: Broadman & Holman, 1999), 153-54.

Chapter 5

1. John MacArthur, *MacArthur New Testament Commentary: 1 Corinthians* (Chicago: Moody Press, 1984), 196.

Chapter 6

1. John F. MacArthur, *The Freedom and Power of Forgiveness* (Wheaton, IL: Crossway, 1998), 7.

2. See Robert Jeffress, *When Forgiveness Doesn't Make Sense* (Colorado Springs: WaterBrook Press, 2000), 226.

3. Paraphrased and quoted from John Ortberg, *Everybody's Normal Till You Get to Know Them* (Grand Rapids: Zondervan, 2003), 158-59.

4. S. I. McMillen, *None of These Diseases* (Westwood, NJ: Revell, 1963), 74.

5. Robin Casarjian, interview by *New Age Journal* (September/October 1993): 78, quoted in Tim Jackson, *When Forgiveness Seems Impossible* (Grand Rapids: Radio Bible Class, 1994).

6. Lewis B. Smedes, *The Art of Forgiving: When You Need to Forgive and Don't Know How* (New York: Ballantine, 1996), 27.

Chapter 7

1. The Barna Group, "Born Again Christians Just As Likely to Divorce As Are Non-Christians," *The Barna Update*, September 8, 2004, www. barna.org. Accessed July 6, 2005. Used by permission.

2. Philip Yancey, *I Was Just Wondering* (Grand Rapids: Eerdmans, 1989), 174-75, quoted in Charles R. Swindoll, *Hope Again* (Dallas: Word Publishing, 1996), 100.

3. Winnie Stachelberg, quoted in CNN, "Bush wants marriage reserved for heterosexuals," July 31, 2003, www.cnn.com/2003/ALL POLITICS/07/30/bush.gay.marriage.

4. John Piper, *Brothers, We Are Not Professionals: A Plea to Pastors for Radical Ministry* (Nashville: Broadman & Holman, 2002), 248.

5. Philip Yancey, *Rumors of Another World: What on Earth Are We Missing?* (Grand Rapids: Zondervan, 2003), 81.

6. Adapted from Chuck Swindoll, "Truth or Consequences," *Newsbreak* 12, no. 23 (June 14-20, 1992). Published by First Evangelical Free Church of Fullerton, CA. Used by permission of Charles R. Swindoll.

Chapter 8

1. Analysis of research studies by David Larson, summarized in Philip Yancey, *Finding God in Unexpected Places* (New York: Ballantine, 1995), 82-83.

Chapter 9

1. Mark Buchanan, *Things Unseen: Living in Light of Forever* (Sisters, OR: Multnomah, 2002), 66.

2. Bill Hybels, *Courageous Leadership* (Grand Rapids: Zondervan, 2002), 23.

Chapter 10

1. Statistics from the Christian and Missionary Alliance Stewardship Web Links page, "General Economic and Demographic Facts," www.cmalliance.org/ncm/stewardship/facts.isp.

2. Randy Alcorn, *The Treasure Principle* (Sisters, OR: Multnomah, 2001), 26.

3. Based on an illustration that appeared in Greg Lafferty, "Right on the Money," *Preaching Today* (2002): 3.

4. Richard Leider, quoted in David Jeremiah, *Life Wide Open: Unleashing the Power of a Passionate Life* (Brentwood, TN: Integrity Publishers, 2003), 23-24.

5. John Eldredge, *Wild at Heart: Discovering the Passionate Soul of a Man* (Nashville: Nelson, 2001), 142.

6. Paraphrased from Jeremiah, *Life Wide Open*, 103-4.

7. Paraphrased from Jeremiah, *Life Wide Open*, 104.

8. Paraphrased from Jeremiah, *Life Wide Open*, 104.

Chapter 11

1. J. Carl Laney, "The Biblical Practice of Church Discipline," *Bibliotheca Sacra* 143, no. 572 (October–December 1986): 353.

2. Ted G. Kitchens, "Perimeters of Corrective Church Discipline," *Bibliotheca Sacra* 148, no. 590 (April–June 1991): 201.

3. Haddon Robinson, quoted in Mark R. Littleton, "Church Discipline: A Remedy for What Ails the Body," *Christianity Today* 25, no. 9 (May 8, 1981): 31.

4. Marlin Jeschke, *Disciplining the Brother* (Scottdale, PA: Herald, 1972), 14, quoted in George B. Davis, "Whatever Happened to Church Discipline," *Criswell Theological Review* 1, no. 2 (Spring 1987): 349.

5. John White, "The Discipline That Heals," *Moody Monthly* 78, no. 6 (February 1978): 57.

6. Jeschke, *Disciplining the Brother*, 181-82, quoted in Davis, "Whatever Happened to Church Discipline," 354.

7. J. Carl Laney, *A Guide to Church Discipline* (Minneapolis: Bethany House, 1985), 14, quoted in Laney, "The Biblical Practice of Church Discipline," 354.

8. Charles G. Finney, *Lectures to Professing Christians* (New York: Revell, 1878), 61, quoted in J. Carl Laney, "Church Discipline: Rebuilding the Family Fellowship," *Plumb Line* (n.d.): 2.

Chapter 12

1. Ted G. Kitchens, "Perimeters of Corrective Church Discipline," *Bibliotheca Sacra* 148, no. 590 (April–June 1991): 202.

2. See William Barclay, *The Gospel of Matthew*, 2 vols. (Philadelphia: Westminster, 1958), 2, 206, quoted in George B. Davis, "Whatever Happened to Church Discipline," *Criswell Theological Review* 1, no. 2 (Spring 1987): 346-47.

3. Mark R. Littleton, "Church Discipline: A Remedy for What Ails the Body," *Christianity Today* 25, no. 9 (May 8, 1981): 33.

Chapter 13

1. Story taken from a personal Web page, "Daily Celebrations," August 7, 2002, www.dailycelebrations.com/080702.htm.

2. Philippe Petit and John Reddy, "Two Towers, I Walk," *Reader's Digest*, April 1975, 226-27.

3. Denise Banderman, "Professor Takes Students' Test for Them," *Preaching Today*, March 10, 2003, www.preachingtoday.com.

4. Dallas Willard, *The Divine Conspiracy: Rediscovering Our Hidden Life in God* (San Francisco: HarperSanFrancisco, 1998), 38.

5. Willard, *The Divine Conspiracy*, 283.

6. Paraphrased and quoted from Philip Yancey, *Reaching for the Invisible God: What Can We Expect to Find?* (Grand Rapids: Zondervan, 2000), 227-28.

Also available
from **Robert Jeffress**

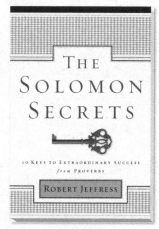

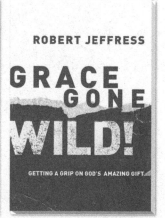